Jealousy

JEALOUSY

True Stories of Love's Favorite Decoy

MARCIANNE BLÉVIS

TRANSLATED BY OLIVIA HEAL

OTHER PRESS · NEW YORK

Ouvrage publié avec le concours du Ministère français chargé de la
Culture—Centre national du livre.
This work has been published with the support of the Centre
National du Livre of the French Ministry of Culture.

Production Editor: Yvonne E. Cárdenas

Book design: Simon M. Sullivan

This book was set in 11 pt Fairfield by Alpha Design & Composition
of Pittsfield, NH.

10 9 8 7 6 5 4 3 2 1

Library of Congress Cataloging-in-Publication Data

Blévis, Marcianne.
[Jalousie. English]
Jealousy : true stories of love's favorite decoy / Marcianne Blévis ; translated by
Olivia Heal.
p. cm.
ISBN 978-1-59051-257-9
1. Jealousy. I. Title.
BF575.J4B5413 2008
152.4'8—dc22   2008019899

CONTENTS

Jealousy

INTRODUCTION

But jealous souls will not be answered so;
They are not ever jealous for the cause.
But jealous for they are jealous;
'tis a monster begot upon itself, born on itself.
— William Shakespeare, *Othello*

Jealousy is unmistakable. It hurts. As *The Oxford English Dictionary* describes it, jealousy is a state of mind arising from the "suspicion, apprehension, or knowledge of rivalry" and affects our body before it reaches the mind. Our best poets have not missed the physical sting of jealousy. Milton speaks of it as the "injured lover's hell," Dryden calls it "jaundice of the soul," and Shakespeare, "the green-ey'd monster." French moralist La Rochefoucauld adds: "Jealousy lives upon doubts. It becomes madness or ceases entirely as soon as we pass from doubt to certainty." From all accounts, jealousy seems to be an apt response to an impending disaster. But why does a jealous individual call upon such a painful mental device to protect himself? Jealousy cannot possibly be a human aberration. And what is the appeal of such a dreadful feeling that sticks to a person like a second skin? It seems to answer some fundamental yearnings.

Although jealousy's torments may drive some people to seek psychological help, an addiction to this thrilling malady is not easily cured. Many of us assume that it is normal to be jealous when we love. After all, one doesn't plan to be jealous. It happens.

Jealousy springs without warning, making a man doubt his worth and charm. He loses his bearings, and the world around him suddenly shrinks. "She didn't pick up her cell phone, yet she knew it was me!" he says of his girlfriend. When a jealous man starts on the course of this powerful emotion he becomes entranced; he can't let go. Jealousy becomes a thrill whose excitement he both seeks and dreads.

Jealous individuals are a challenge for psychoanalysts. The analyst must travel with the patient in uncertain spaces, full of ambushes and traps, relying on her compass to bring the patient to the point where he can accept that jealousy is but a stand-in for a moment when he was deprived of love's sustenance. An antidote to despair, jealousy is better than feeling nothing. It would not cross the jealous man's mind, as he rants and raves, that the culprit is neither his lover nor his rival, but a moment in his history that wrecked his hopes and damaged his trust in himself and in those he loves.

This is a book about people, like you and me, who have been struck by the hellish wand of jealousy, at one time or another. These people have careers, lead normal lives, and are very keen to understand their plight. Their stories show that if jealousy usually erupts in the midst of a love affair, jealousy is not a measure of love, or one of its necessary components. The appeal of jealousy is bound up with one's identity, one's sense of self. It reverts to a time in childhood or adolescence when the person was left wanting the kind of erotic and loving responses that would have made him feel strong, autonomous, and desirable. Jealousy, therefore, can be seen as a delayed reaction to a situation that left a person helpless and humiliated.

The heroes and heroines of the chapters that follow amply demonstrate that jealousy has much to do with a need to control the mental landscape of one's partners, as if the jealous person's survival depends on it. The jealous man embarks on a love affair like a colonizer driven to preempt any attempt of escape or secret plots to overthrow him. Under the circumstances, of course, the loved one's word is no guarantee! The jealous person is unable to trust anything. He doubts, suspects, or imagines extraordinary scenarios of deception, waiting for the other shoe to drop. Eventually, reality catches up with his theater of illusions and his mistaken definition of love. He can't know or guess everything. It is obvious that his lover can never become totally transparent to him. Every human being needs her privacy, her secret garden. Yet for the jealous person, this state of affairs is intolerable. He needs total control over his subjects.

Much of the difficulty of treating a jealous individual stems from the fact that he can't see or imagine what life would be without jealousy. When he is jealous, his vision of the world becomes impaired. It is as if he strains to look at his loved one through the slats of a Venetian blind. His lover, unlike him, is free to see and desire as she pleases. Unfettered by jealousy's chains, she appears to him as if magically unreachable. His gaze unreciprocated, he feels deprived of attention, respect, and love, left to brood over his terrible fate. He is reduced to being a private eye. At the same time, he is ill equipped to distinguish an effective betrayal from a simple fiction born of his anguish. Yet more often than not, he understands nothing. Ravaged, yet burned with desire, he errs endlessly in jealousy's labyrinth, incapable of finding an exit. He can neither truly love nor truly hate. He wavers between the two, harassing his partner, who ultimately has no other choice but to fulfill his direst predictions and depart.

Other times the jealous person uses jealousy to fuel his passion, as if a peaceful relationship is synonymous with death.

When something feels amiss, jealousy's implacable logic convinces him that his sentiment is perfectly justified, and so his tired passion is awakened yet again. It is as if jealousy is filling a gap. He may even fall back in love with an ex-partner when such a person has a new love interest. As a whole, however, jealousy is rarely triggered by a lover's actual betrayal. The jealous man is usually alone on jealousy's stage, and it is with great reluctance that he allows his analyst to take part in the play. While he desperately yearns to be rescued, he resists the hand eager to pull him out of his misery.

There are no recipes to effectively cure jealousy because its roots are inscribed in the particular circumstances of one's personal history. However, although no story resembles another, there is much to learn from the stories of jealous men and women in agony. Jealousy takes a person by surprise and then stuns him. In order to soothe the crisis he endlessly revisits the scene of the "crime" in search of an explanation, torn between his desire to inculpate or exonerate the "suspect." Yet the answer he seeks is not in the here and now. The path to recovery demands a shift in perspective. Usually a chance event, an unexpected outburst, or a violent reaction to an insignificant detail displaces jealousy onto the terrain where it first served its purpose. If there is suspense in jealousy, there is also suspense in the sessions of a jealous patient. An analyst must seize the moment, and not hesitate to bring the original trauma into view. Through the relationship between analyst and patient, the patient experiences the twists and turns that bring jealousy back to its home base. Jealousy looms large in what makes us human. Therefore we can gain a greater understanding of crucial moments in our lives if we examine them through jealousy's lens.

This is not a book for psychiatric professionals. Although I'm both a psychiatrist and a psychoanalyst, my intent in this book is to share with readers insights gleaned from my experiences in dealing with the rigid convictions of jealous patients. The task of sorting out the muddle that makes up the painful moments of a patient's history can prove daunting. Jealousy is a hard nut to crack and demands patience, determination, and staying power. The discoveries the analyst makes are not scripted illustrations of psychological theories but rather they emerge from the field, so to speak. The analyst, when dealing with the torments of jealousy, is not merely a compass guiding the patient out of his misery. She must risk entering into a world of violence and passion and carve herself a place where she can be heard so as to break jealousy's spell.

Each chapter in this book revolves around the story of a particular individual and explains along the way the different facets of jealousy and how they originate. Chapter 1, for example, details how jealousy is a torture that people inflict not only on themselves but also on those closest to them. Jealous individuals want to crawl inside the minds of their friends and partners as if to rob them of their existence and joy. Chapter 5, on brothers and sisters, looks at the different ways jealousy actually enriches relationships with siblings. Other chapters show the connection between jealousy and traumatic events that have been expelled from memory. In chapter 6, for instance, readers meet David, a man who curiously never felt jealous until he was able to uncover a family secret. Paula, in chapter 7, was wildly jealous of her lovers and could never stop searching their pockets. Only when she recovered her lost femininity could she let go of her extreme jealousy. Finally chapter 10 provides the most surprising story in the book, that of George, the man who was jealous of the bouquet of flowers in my office. Separated from his mother at a young age, he used the flowers as a go-between to connect again with his mother's radiance and love.

Jealousy is indeed love's favorite decoy. This is why it is so hard to overcome. These stories amply demonstrate how both men and women revert to jealousy when they lack the emotional tools to tackle the mysteries of love and erotic desire. Yet to relinquish jealousy offers a whole new lease on life and a new capacity to love.

CHAPTER I

SIMON: THE DEEPLY JEALOUS BOYFRIEND

Simon was a twenty-nine-year-old commodities trader who came to see me because his girlfriend, tired of his constant accusations, was threatening to leave him. "I am going to prove you right if you keep harassing me," she told him. Simon, in a rare moment of lucidity, was beginning to realize that his behavior made him repulsive to her.

Simon telephoned his girlfriend constantly and invented numerous excuses to see her at work. For him, as for other jealous people, the cell phone is a godsend! He now had an umbilical cord that monitored her every action. He couldn't bear for her to live one instant without him. "I have to be continuously linked to her," he affirmed. "I can't cope with not being able to join her when she is in a meeting or when she turns off her cell to be out of reach." His sweetheart was not allowed breathing room, to have a thought to herself, or simply a bit of privacy. "Do I have to wait for her death to know where to find her? At least in death, I'll be sure that she is not thinking about another man!" he cried.

Many jealous individuals have similar death wishes for their lovers and believe their turmoil will end when the object of their attention disappears. "Jealousy is always born with love but does not always die with it," wrote La Rochefoucauld.

Everything outside of Simon's grasp awakened his jealousy. Even his partner's previous affairs provided him with proof for the continuous case of infidelity he built against her. Both judge and plaintiff, Simon always found his girlfriend guilty.

He also inevitably suspected his lover of concealing something from him. Nothing seemed to appease his desire to know what she felt. Ready to give his suspicions free rein at the slightest excuse, Simon seemed to enjoy gathering evidence of hypothetical infidelities. He cultivated the art of jotting down confessions and didn't hesitate to torture his girlfriend with exhausting interrogations. If jealous people are so difficult to bear, is it because they are sadistic?

Sadism and jealousy

At first glance, the jealous individual appears to follow the teachings of the controversial eighteenth-century philosopher Marquis de Sade. "I have the right to possess you totally," Sade wrote. Yet the jealous lover is incapable of being a sadist. According to Sade, a lover may consider another's body as goods at the community's disposal. In addition, Sade defined amorous relations as violent reciprocity, which were in his eyes revolutionary. Jealousy, with its desire for control and domination, was therefore perceived as a by-product of outdated bourgeois attitudes. In that sense Sade's vision of the world aimed to eradicate passion and, by the same token, the woes of love.

The sadism of the jealous person, therefore, turns out to be the reverse of the one advocated by Sade. It is the fact that love *cannot* be controlled that causes the jealous person such anguish and fits of rage.

THE DESIRE FOR DOMINATION

Simon's desire for domination and control affected quite a number of issues in his life and were directly linked to his jealousy. For example, when he refused to satisfy his companion's erotic desire, because it wasn't based on his own initiative, he uttered that he was a "man, a real man" and, moreover, that his lover's surge of desire was completely out of control and intolerable to him. Simon was jealous of his partner's spontaneous impulses, which were dangerous to him. For a jealous individual like Simon, every surprise was a source of displeasure. If he couldn't master desire's upsurge, it frightened him.

Analysis made Simon recognize that he gave the same rebuff to anyone who asked something of him—whatever it might be, even to buy a pack of cigarettes. He felt threatened by another person's desires. Anything that he couldn't fully control distressed him. This character trait became clearer when he and I linked it back to the jealous rivalry he experienced whenever his partner wanted her own space or freedom.

One incident was particularly telling. Having spent several days at some friends' house in the country, Simon could not leave the place without taking, unbeknownst to his hosts, an object that in his eyes belonged to him by right. "Nothing big, just a little souvenir!" he said. The object in question was not precious, but Simon felt he had a right to demand something. Was this a simple craving? No, because the object had little value. The act of stealing it was more important to him.

Simon helped himself to other people's things because, unconsciously, he was jealous of the people with whom he rubbed shoulders. It was his jealousy that provoked this desire to steal, not his desire for the object. As jealous types of this kind are tragically lacking their own identities, they live vicariously, feeding off others. They appropriate an object like cannibals devour their enemies, in order to gain power for themselves. They believe that through the act of theft (or devouring) they are incorporating the qualities of those they secretly admire. Simon looked for a "little something, a little souvenir" in his friends' house so that he might get hold of the immaterial, imaginary part, which, in his eyes, constituted the inestimable treasure of the place.

THE EVERYDAY LIFE OF JEALOUSY

Simon behaved very differently when his companion was down or depended on him for something. Only then did his anxiety seem to lessen. "If she needs me, she won't escape me," he believed. But as soon as she demonstrated well-being, he wanted to obliterate the feeling. "If she revels in her own pleasures, she is independent and excludes me." For jealous individuals the domain of the other is one of treachery. Simon's jealousy seemed to find an outlet when he could make himself useful; he then was calm again. Not through kindness, however, but because his need for domination over his lover was satisfied. Simon was helpful only when he defined the terms of his assistance.

A jealous person like Simon will not bring the pack of cigarettes one asks for, but rather impose three boxes of cigars! Wearying and harassing in his rigidity, he gives us a glimpse of how jealousy is the expression of an unquenchable desire to dominate every wish for autonomy that his companions—be they friends or lovers—might voice.

Many forms of aggression in everyday life are rooted in jealousy. When Simon's lover told him about something, for instance, Simon seemed interested for a moment or two before quickly becoming scornful, which had no other aim than to make what she liked undesirable. On other occasions, he unconsciously borrowed certain themes or ideas from his girlfriend, claiming responsibility for them, before complaining of his partner's (legitimate!) protest. In this case, imitating the other—robbing or denigrating her ideas—always comes back to the same point: through his will to dominate, a jealous person sucks the life out of those he thinks he loves.

Jealousy at its roots is always the same: Simon, like all jealous people, couldn't stand the idea that the one he loved could be interested in things that excluded him. She was not allowed to be autonomous, to have a secret garden of her own. Behaving perfectly when his companion was unhappy, Simon showed a frank and incomprehensible bitterness when his loved one improved.

Simon, full of concern, had accompanied his best friend to the hospital, but when he caught sight of the elegant clothes the latter had packed—a way of fighting his declining health—he grudgingly marveled over them. His friend's strong desire to live, displayed through taking such care, was intolerable to Simon because it was outside his control. If his friend didn't owe him anything, then his friend was free. Jealous people want to control the lives of those they mix with, as if the idea of free will were a personal offense. One can then understand why they are always on the hunt for proof of the other's infidelity. The stakes are effectively life or death if the partner manages to escape into her own autonomous existence instead of being at his service.

The freeloader's anguish

Simon wanted to subsume his lover by closely watching all her apparent wishes to escape him. He overflowed with rage when his desire for domination was squelched. Faced with the failure of his authoritarian power, he erupted, ready to destroy the relationship rather than endure an affront.

The hostility in the jealous individual comes from the fact that his desire for domination is not satisfied. His sense of self is under siege. As a result, the jealous man, who no longer knows who he is or where he is, masks his envy and lives like a parasite off another's desire. In order to restore his feelings of existence, he wants to be tightly knit to the one he loves and refuses to be severed from her even by mere thought.

Ultimately, one can never be truly sheltered in a haven stolen from another. Simon couldn't stop panicking, for example, every time his lover left him to follow her own desires. Simon also foresaw that a rival would eventually steal his refuge from him.

Such parasitic behavior made it impossible for Simon to stabilize his identity as a man. His desire for domination was equal to his uncertainties. In the end, Simon's rival was the desire that he encountered in his loved one. His strategies of control, used to ensure his mental survival, only guaranteed a vicious cycle of self-destructiveness.

Betrayal

As Simon's analyst I was not spared his suspicion that I too could betray him by favoring other patients over him. It was clear to me that Simon treated me just like he treated his father who he said preferred his older son over Simon. Simon's parents had adopted this child before Simon was born. The boy was the son of the father's deceased brother. This adoption had never been clearly spelled out by the family, thus making it impossible for Simon to have a normal relationship with his brother or his father. He felt compelled to love his older brother but also sensed that he was not allowed to compete with him or to jeopardize his position in the family. As a result, he felt separated from his father who he thought used the older brother as a shield against

Simon's own craving for intimacy with him. For Simon, therefore, his father was untouchable. And, for a boy, nothing is harder to bear than a father who deliberately avoids intimacy with one son in order to protect another. This betrayal was consequently projected onto all of Simon's relationships including his with me. Everyone was susceptible to betraying him one day. Therefore, he felt entitled to take from others what he felt so deprived of, that share of intimacy symbolized by the objects he occasionally stole.

One day Simon did something unexpected. He canceled a session with me. A few hours before his scheduled time, though, he called to say that he was feeling terrible and wanted to come anyway. I obliged him and quickly found out that he had canceled his session only to test me. He needed to make sure that I had not given his hour to someone else. He had a dream the night before in which I was the conductor of a train that he couldn't enter. I told him that I did not replace him with anyone and that he had been right to call. Moreover, I was not unreachable and he should feel free to get in touch with me as long as he needed to. This exchange allowed him to grasp his deep desire to be in touch with his father and his craving for his real presence and involvement. The experience of reliving his desire to connect to his father opened for Simon a whole new perspective not only on his childhood but on his life in the here and now. He realized that what he did not dare ask his father directly he was able to get from me: he had his own place and no one could take it away from him. He understood for the first time that intimacy and closeness are not goods to be stolen from others but exist in their own right if he cares to look for them.

Past betrayals, thefts, and dark secrets exist in many family histories, and when they remain under cover, they continue to tarnish the lives of children and grandchildren, eating away at their senses of identity and self-worth. To unearth the past takes courage because it requires questioning situations that would be more comfortable to leave unexamined. This is not about shifting the blame but rather about ceasing to be taken hostage by past occurrences. Uncovering the past does not incriminate, but rather it can afford a measure of freedom.

CHAPTER 2

CHLOE'S STRUGGLE WITH A CHOICE OF WORDS

Chloe, a refined and soft-spoken thirty-year-old editor at a woman's magazine, came to analysis for a reason that is both urgent and common: she had recently met a man. Although her new lover said nothing particularly unsettling, she felt suddenly seized with panic by his choice of words. An alarming attack of anxiety had taken hold and plunged her into an abyss from which she couldn't find her way out. Chloe was overwhelmed with thoughts she considered insane. She was, essentially, being torn apart by an intense jealousy, which was all the more painful because she couldn't figure out its source. But this wasn't the first time she had felt the claws of this monster. Up until the time she came to see me, she had always disguised her jealousy in seemingly legitimate justifications. This time, however, it had become impossible for her to lie to herself any longer; she couldn't blame such a groundless jealousy on anyone but herself.

Without any preconceived ideas, I tried to map out a blueprint of the thoughts and sensations that preceded Chloe's jealous outburst. I set about questioning her about the words, thoughts, and images that preceded this surge of anxious panic. "I all but passed out with pain," she explained, "when he murmured into my ear: 'You'll never know how much I would have loved you.' You see how sensitive I am to grammar!" She adds, with a certain irony in her voice, "My jealousy came simply from his use of the conditional perfect tense at that very moment. It's crazy, isn't it? I couldn't stay in his presence, it was as if I was being repelled by a powerful magnet." An avalanche of suspicions instantly fell over her. "With whom will he talk about me in the past tense? To which woman will he direct these words, once I've disappeared from his life?" Chloe nervously interrogated herself, and her jealousy erupted over this hypothetical future rival. "I spend my time terrified, waiting for him to have an encounter, as I did during my previous relationships. It seems to me that the future is lined with traps and pitfalls. I fear every other woman, no matter who, as any one of them could, at any moment, seduce him and turn him away from me. It's hell!" Sensing that she was about to hit rock bottom, she asked for my help.

THE CONFUSION OF FEELINGS

In her life, Chloe wavered anxiously between desire and anguish. She couldn't settle between the assurance of being loved and that of being neglected. She didn't know if she was truly herself or if she had become a stranger in her own reality. It was not surprising, then, that she was sensitive to the grammar of her lover's words as well as their meaning. By intertwining the past and hypothetical future to the conditional perfect, her lover seemed to suggest that he no longer shared the present moment with her. In this case, her jealousy arose from a few simple words in which abandonment was at once affirmed and denied. In the intimacy of their embrace, his confession—uttered in this manner—took on the meaning of a foretold death. Chloe received it like a stab in the chest.

As a result, she no longer knew who she was: the woman loved in the present or the woman forgotten in the future. She no longer recognized her lover, the man who pledged his love to her. Despite believing herself safe in his embrace, Chloe felt estranged from herself and thrust into a state of terrible anguish. Words no longer served to secure her identity. Instead, they left her in a state of vertigo, unable to pin down the meaning of the statement and its paradoxical formulation. Her lover's use of this ambivalent tense could have been interpreted as just a clumsy attempt to master the unreliability of every relationship or even as a sign of an unconscious tentativeness. In other words, Chloe could have used it as an excuse to get angry with her lover or to accuse him of insincerity. But having lost all ability to react, she instead found herself constrained and destitute.

Faced with a loss of confidence, she became unable to pin down the threat, to size it up, and to defend herself against it. Both her lover and her hypothetical rival had become overpowering figures. Distressed, Chloe gave her lover's words the weight of a fatal verdict that further intensified her anxiety. Jealousy is a torture that nourishes itself on the slightest words, twisting them to its own advantage. Once she was in its clutches, the ambiguities of language became exhibits in her lover's case— evidently against him.

Concealed behind Chloe's jealous exterior existed a tremendous fear that left her defenseless. Her lover's use of ambiguous rhetoric had clearly upset her. Insightful on other occasions, she found herself completely powerless in this conversation and felt herself become stupid and pathetic, while her lover appeared out of reach, as if his turn of phrase had made him as inaccessible as he was incomprehensible.

If we are to believe jealous men and women, their suspicions of others are at the root of their panic. Yet, since Chloe's jealousy was sparked *after* the troubled conversation, she demonstrated how anxiety actually incites jealousy. In other words, jealousy masked a terror that left Chloe speechless. As if pulled into another space and time, Chloe no longer knew how to return to the present. That is, jealousy attempted to make sense of an anxiety that was triggered by her lover's muddled messages. Presence and absence were enunciated as though they were the same. "How can it be that at the very moment when he tells me he loves me, he speaks as though we were no longer together?" she marveled.

OUT OF REACH

This fit of anguish opened up a gulf between Chloe and her lover, as if he had ceased to belong to the same species. She no longer saw him as he was, but rather, in her eyes he took on an imposing stance and was transformed into a profoundly cruel human being. From that point on, Chloe, as if famished, turned every word inside out in order to discover some hidden message. Under these conditions, her lover's words essentially became indecipherable predictions, which drove Chloe to question herself on how best to behave so as not to displease him. The jealous type falls prey to interior battles—primarily a war with personal demons—as exhausting as they are futile. Whereas one woman might believe her rival knows how to satisfy the demands of her lover better than she can, another woman will imagine that her rival is adorned with a mysterious charm that only she possesses. Jealous men and women forget that they are the only ones to bestow their rivals with so many favorable attributes.

Chloe couldn't have been less aware of how much she deprived herself of her feminine distinctions in the shadow of this phantom. Shrinking before any woman, she should have realized the evidence: her rival didn't exist.

In showing herself to be so sensitive to the grammar of her lover's statement, Chloe invites us into the thin cracks between words, giving us access to the little girl inside, who was long ago uprooted and disoriented when faced with her own passionate urges. Was she torn from the childhood power to love freely by a great fear of being rejected?

Almost without exception, every jealous person finds herself possessed by the fatality of language. It is because of this that jealousy often appears to verge on lunacy, reminding us that deep inside there resides an unfathomable terror—passionate excitement is but the mask. Like Chloe, jealous men and women always seem to be painfully pushed outside of themselves, waiting to be understood.

A LANDSCAPE OF RUINS

In order to weave together the loose threads of a damaged psychological fabric, one has to allow the reasons behind the disaster to emerge from childhood. The psychoanalyst's flexibility is called upon when he or she climbs into the patient's childhood skin—to imagine this skin and to find the missing words. Rather than let myself wander through the twists and turns of Chloe's jealous assumptions, I followed my own questions about the paradoxical emotions of attraction and rejection that she had experienced at the most intense point of her anguish, which was just before her confusion changed into suspicion:

> An image that comes to me during my sleepless nights returned.
> In a city devastated by a war or bombing, a stray dog, starved and
> skin and bone, walks the length of a facade of a ruined building,
> half-fallen-down, which is strangely glowing in the night. This
> starved stray dog, I know it's me. Me when I'm unhappy.

This image, born at the place where dream meets daydream, seemed to condense various important elements. At a crossroads, Chloe put us in touch with an age-old anguish (the solitary march of the animal in the night), the child's former attempts at making sense of her chaos (the dog, skin and bone and "starved"), and her desire to take care of herself. These images recurred as both an appeal for help and a testimony of her tenacity. I saw a message in this narrative coming from Chloe-the-starved addressed to Chloe-the-jealous. Her appeal could not go unnoticed, nor could I exempt myself from deciphering it with her.

In this reverie, elements from her past (wars and bombings) associated themselves with the present situation (an issue regarding her lover).

The glowing facades made me think of the faces or expressions that every child scrutinizes, the facades of those who surrounded her. Did Chloe not examine her lover with eyes and ears as an alert baby would? I let the images she had described form themselves in my mind: the emaciated dog, her own self, a baby and a stray, lost in a universe of facades, devastated by a war and bombing. The word selected for this strange nocturnal light—*glow*—suggested that the facades were for a moment glowing before falling into ruin during the shattered nights of insomnia.

As a child, had Chloe secretly, avidly looked at the glowing and excessively delighted faces of her father and mother, allowing herself to imagine sexual passion? Had she not also been affected by their wars, as the abyss of suffering incited by her lover's grammatical blunder suggested? The bombings rumbled, the parents raised their furious voices in anger, at once enigmatic and terrifying. I tried to repair the gap between the two languages (that of the child and that of the adults) delineated by the words *war* and *bombing*.

I pointed out to Chloe that she had doubtlessly perceived some-thing in her lover's face that echoed the duality of his words. I questioned her about both the intimate and the actual war (World War II) experienced by her parents—the meeting points of the large and small histories, hers and those close to her. What con-flict could have been the cause of these ruins, these face-facades that she watched with her eyes open wide, starved to know where she stood? Behind all her dreams of love and jealousy, it was this questioning that seemed to insistently repeat itself.

THE SECRET FACADES

Visibly surprised by my questions, Chloe began to tell me about her family wars, the one in which her father had disappeared as well as the one her parents had fought before World War II. She knew that her mother had been betrayed by her father for rea-sons as uncertain as they were sudden. Her husband's death had led to the desperate collapse of this woman, who, from then on, never again spoke to her daughter about him. Despite this heavy silence, Chloe had kept several photos of her father that she used to look at in private. The glowing faces (facades) that reveal the loving passion between her father and mother, the ruined faces after their disputes, the collapsed face of her sad mother, and the silence surrounding her father's sudden death during the war—a subject the little girl had thought one must never speak of on pain of death—all mapped out the child's landscape. These issues continued to cause insomnia, intense anguish, or very painful attacks of jealousy because Chloe-the-starved, faced with an unresolved past, had muzzled her legitimate worries.

Children look at what is shown to them (the facades), but they also look for the unsaid or the suggested (hidden behind these facades). The image of the dog walking along the ruins, starved of words, evokes these flawed perceptions. The face-facade of her lover, combined with his ambiguous message, had revived all of Chloe's unanswered questions. The chance usage of the ambiguous conditional perfect tense had recalled those contradictory messages she had once received: seeing but seeing nothing, knowing but pretending to know nothing, being present but not being there. Chloe's jealousy kept her in this identical situation of suspense.

While her mother withdrew into a hostile silence, the little girl was deprived of that necessary shared time and space of mourning; her loss was not allowed to produce legitimate tears. Instead it became a ghost that could not be translated into words and feelings nor could it find representation in dreams. Removed and cut off from the external world behind her ruined and mute face, this mother had left her "stray" daughter on the outside. Also, never having heard her mother speak of her father romantically, Chloe was not given the opportunity to learn about love. She was therefore unable to explore the reality of her emotions. She placed all of her expectations in her lover, hoping that he would give her access to this part of herself—thus rendering the terrain particularly sensitive. The slightest discrepancies in vocabulary could, under these conditions, cause a rift. Chloe's jealousy drove her to imagine a woman to whom her beloved would address himself once he had forgotten about her. She felt tortured just thinking about it.

Deprived of words by her mother, Chloe was suspended between her two parents, between an active and a passive femininity, between the language of childhood and that of adulthood. Her jealousy was evidence of an impossible tension between love and anguish. On the one hand, she wavered between the desire to be loved and recognized as a woman and, on the other, she felt terror about her amorous urges. Her indissoluble jealousy repeatedly expressed something that had to remain unspeakable and secret.

BEHIND THE CARNIVAL MASK

A psychoanalyst's hypotheses aren't pertinent unless they help the patient relive the scraps of her past that she can remember despite repression, censorship, or denial. A psychoanalyst gives life back to all the traces and meanings of lived events that have remained gagged and bound in the psyche as dangerous enigmas. Just as an historian attempts to give words back to the dead in order to resuscitate them, the psychoanalyst goes into the space of transference, searching through the patient's words for memories that have been muzzled or frozen in order to reactivate them.

Chloe responded to my hypothesis that her love and anguish were one and the same by telling me about her dream.

> I pass a man on the street who is wearing a carnival mask, like those they wear in Venice—hard, small, narrow, and closed. Some sort of terrifying beaked rostrum. I am told he's a pope of the Renaissance. I have to make love to him. I feel as though I'm a baby, although, in the dream, I'm an adult; I become intensely aroused, but strangely experience no pleasure.

The pope wears a mask that is hard and disturbing. A terrifying rostrum deforms his face, leading me to think that Chloe may have caught an indecipherable expression on her father's face. By reviving agonizing images that were up until then unspeakable, the dream awakens the memory of this terrifying expression: a carnival mask, closed and incomprehensible. Regarding the term *renaissance*, this reminded Chloe of the novelty of a new relationship. All of these elements of the dream—the disturbing character, his hidden face, the sexual delight (which recalls the glowing light of the facades)—plunged her into a traumatic time in which terror and excessive delight mixed with one another. The unspeakable secret had at last found words and images. Once shared with her analyst, it stopped being so dangerous.

Chloe feared seeing in her father's face an inadmissible feeling: something closed and hard like the mask of the Renaissance pope of her dream. A similar facial expression would probably have signified scolding, punishment, and neglect in the child's eyes. Her lover's phrase, "you'll never know how much I would have loved you," came, without her knowing, out of the mouth of the same hard face—the face of her fears—reviving the ancient enigma that had formerly disoriented her. At the time of his death, Chloe's father had played an essential role in preventing the child from being sucked into the downward spiral of her mother's collapse. Chloe vowed an unconditional love to him that she knew was forbidden. If an impulse in childhood is struck down by a prohibition, it transforms itself into terror and anguish. Wasn't Chloe's love for her father—a source of life for her—smothered by her mother, causing her to transform both her love and her feeling full of life into guilt? Jealousy and guilt then united to destroy her relationships, revealing that they originated in her fear of loving a man. The analysis worked by removing these prohibitions, by outwitting the terror they harbored. It provided a space for desire, and in this way each session of Chloe's analysis was a renaissance, a rebirth.

For Chloe's father, the birth of his daughter also represented a renaissance in the life of the couple and the world. Yes, her father had also been unhappy, like her, but not because of her. She understood that, for her father and mother, her birth was a claim to life as she came into the world in the middle of the war. Her passion for her lover thus seemed to have awakened inexplicably the sounds of war and the din of prohibited love (not only her parents' bliss that she watched in secret, but also her craving for her dead father who was persona non grata in her mother's eyes), as well as the desire to live and love despite it all. Jealousy not only tangles our memories, but also puts us in contact with those unconscious forces of childhood that are struggling to free themselves from the realm of the incommunicable.

Chloe was unable to mourn her father as long as he was held in silence where her mother had buried him. Didn't the glowing facades remind her of how much, in untroubled times, their faces had glowed with happiness before falling to ruin? This loss, screened by her jealousy, was colored with nostalgia.

MEMORY'S SINKING SANDS

The attacks of rage, provoked by her lover's betrayals—be they real or imagined—attempted to at last define the contours of her father's love for her and hers for her father. Chloe had forgotten everything about her father, even the memory of his face. Her jealousy was at once a prohibition (she was not allowed to love because she was not allowed to love her father) and a call to free love from its straitjacket (she refused to be abandoned and reduced to silence).

Awakened from her jealous spell, she could allow her immense love for her father to be reborn without further anguish. Up until then, in each of her encounters, the slightest hypothetical retreat of her partners had signified both abandonment and forbidden complaints.

Chloe's jealousy was a ravaging pain that destroyed her relationships, but it was also evidence of the heartache caused by losing her father. The resolution came when she could finally love her father, a man, but also love herself when in love. Her love for her father had been sealed off by her mother's interdiction, whether imagined or real, and by the silence imposed upon her. This resulted in cutting Chloe off from an essential dimension of her feminine identity.

Jealousy is not merely the repeated coming and going between love and anxiety. The anguished fluctuation of the jealous individual between love and destruction, which often results in a permanent state of watching and scrutinizing, is not a disguised form of hostility, but is altogether of another nature. A jealous person effectively reproaches her lover for not managing to cure her by satisfying her need to be loved, and particularly by not recognizing the intensity of her love. Chloe's real complaint therefore concerned the impossibility of recalling the memory of a forbidden love in her childhood. Thus the demand of the jealous individual, separated from her past, was impossible to fulfill.

The psychoanalyst, by reconnecting the patient with her childhood, can therefore intervene where a lover can't. Chloe rediscovered a space of freedom the day she understood that her passionate excitement was but a pale reflection of the intense attention she had received from her father and that she had been forced, under her mother's command, to forget. She once again claimed the right to love madly, wildly, without sinking into anguish at the slightest grammatical discrepancy. She then began to love (rightly or wrongly) all sorts of conjugations.

CHAPTER 3

FRANK: THE MAN TORMENTED BY RIVALS

Frank was suffering the first time he came to my office. He had just learned that his former girlfriend was finding consolation with another man. After returning from a trip, he went to visit her on a whim. Outside her apartment door, he heard an unknown voice—a man's voice—and froze immediately. Later, having waited for the lover to leave, he caught sight of his rival.

Frank was a twenty-seven-year-old lawyer, very thin with good looks and a confident air. I was surprised, though, the next time I saw him. His demeanor had changed. He was tense and preoccupied. He felt absent, he said, from everything that surrounded him. He desired only one thing: to win back his beloved. He no longer understood why he had left her. Did he still love her? Was it the appearance of another man by his sweetheart's side that renewed his love while also awakening his jealousy?

I mentioned this idea to him, but he reproached me for even suggesting it and for not having stopped him from leaving this woman in the first place. It would have been useless to remind him that not so long ago he had stated that he was no longer in love with her. It would also be cruel to point out that he had decided on his own to break off the affair. Furthermore, when he made the decision, he told me that a psychoanalyst should never intervene in the mysteries of love.

Frank appeared to contemplate his life as though it belonged to someone else. He was consumed with scrutinizing a disaster only he could see. He tortured himself during our sessions about when he should call his ex-girlfriend to beg for a meeting. He tirelessly questioned himself, wondering about his lover's new partner. How could she have chosen such an ugly man? Can't she see the difference? Had she told this new lover of her terrible sadness after their separation?

Frank was sure that his former girlfriend still loved him. It couldn't be otherwise.

THE DESPISED RIVAL FIGURE

Readers may think that Frank demonstrated a typical masculine bitterness and that his jealousy was normal. His girlfriend, who failed to nurse an eternal regret, had wounded his self-regard. But in this case, it was not only about self-regard. When a man desires a woman, other men seem to adorn her with mysterious attributes that fuel his rivalry; he envies the person who possesses this desired woman. Freud would have seen in this the trace of every boy's infantile desire: to covet his father's woman.

Frank refused to believe that his love could have been resuscitated purely because another man desired his former, abandoned partner. This refusal was a form of denial. Frank hadn't become truly aware of his loss until another man took his place. Only then, due to his jealousy toward the rival, did Frank recognize the value of his previously deserted ex. It was true, however, that his jealousy was not dictated by an overestimation of this competitor. He knew this man was no better or stronger than he was. Therefore Frank's dilemma was not like a straightforward dispute between a young boy and his father over winning the mother. Beyond a very natural hostility toward his rival, Frank was plagued by a profound confusion: Why did his girlfriend care for a man who was less attractive than he was?

Jealousy and contempt don't ordinarily come together. Indeed, Frank's jealousy revealed that he was more distressed because he couldn't find anything in common with his rival. Without a point of comparison with this new man, Frank seemed to be suspended in a void.

The intensity of his turmoil suggested more than basic antagonism. He, literally, could no longer hold himself together: he fidgeted on the couch and often got up to pace back and forth as if he were filled with insufferable anguish and intolerable thoughts. He felt weightless, so much so that he said he could be sucked under the wheels of a passing car. His body no longer had a center of gravity. He drifted with his thoughts. He said life had no more sense than his body had mass. On the metaphorical set of scales relating him to other men, he weighed nothing—no more than a feather.

"How could she have left me for that loser?" he asked, even though the difference between the two men, which he believed was to his advantage, failed to appease him. Was this merely a narcissistic wound? Unlike many jealous women who deprecate themselves in favor of a rival who becomes, for them, the symbol of femininity, Frank didn't assign his rival particularly flattering masculine attributes. His turmoil seemed to arise from a rift between what he imagined his rival to be and himself, rather than from a comparison. Frank was radically unable to recognize himself in the man, and it was precisely this inability to relate to his rival that caused his profound disorientation. In my view, Frank's problem shed new light on the complex link between jealousy and rivalry.

REVEALING A NARCISSISTIC FLAW

Narcissism or self-love is born from the support we get from those we love or who have loved us. When self-love is not there, we miss that essential backbone of our personality. Only the feeling of a radical betrayal makes us aware that such support is missing. The sense of desertion is intensely painful. The loss of a once-trustworthy support leaves the jealous person unsteady, giving him the feeling of being deceived by the whole world— particularly by those he loves.

It is therefore paramount not to misjudge the emotions behind narcissistic collapse. The rival offers the jealous individual a narcissistic support in preventing a breakdown. Jealous types experience their own bodies as vessels ravaged by a nameless anguish that cannot be attributed solely to amorous rejection, but rather to a breakdown that must have occurred earlier in childhood.

To be jealous of a rival provides the last defense before a major breakdown, but it also provides a source of alienation. To attempt to identify with the rival only provides an illusion of a borrowed body, since the jealous individual cannot trust his own. Yet a borrowed body cannot experience by proxy what it means to be a sexual human being. The rival himself, as successful in love as he may be, cannot quite answer the question that torments the jealous protagonist: What does it mean to live as a man or as a woman? Rivalry offers a painful alternative to this enigma but an unsatisfactory one at that. The mysteries of sexuality are not solved by wishing to live in a rival's shoes but at least it offers an explanation for the feeling of being displaced. Frank failed to find in his rival any point of comparison that would justify his ex-girlfriend's choice.

On the shores of alienation

For a while, Frank spent hours watching the entrance to his former lover's house, finding meaning behind her slightest actions and gestures, rereading her letters. Unsuccessfully, he tried to imagine what his former girlfriend could be doing or saying with this new man at her side. This woman, whom he thought he loved anew, seemed impenetrable to him. She had become a sort of all-powerful goddess holding his life and death in her hands. One could say that his former lover had suddenly become a complete stranger to him. He no longer knew who she was. She represented otherness in its most radical form. He didn't know, and didn't wish to know, that he was the only one who saw her in this way.

For the jealous person, the one he loves is a unique and indecipherable mystery. Jealousy reaches down into that anguish of the very first moments of life when the perfect harmony between mother and child inevitably breaks. Every child listens with open ears, feels with his skin, his eyes wide, to the mother who gives him his first care and attention. Very early on, she seems to be very beautiful. He feels enveloped in her beauty. But the perception of the first signs of dissonance opens a gulf of dreadful mysteries beneath his feet. This anguish does, however, have its virtues. By forcing the child to understand the wants of this other (distinct from himself), the mother turns his gaze outward, toward the world. This is how the child becomes a seeker.

Frank felt invaded by jealousy. Driven outside of himself by his passion, pushed beyond his limits, he was exposed to an alarming distress that took hold of his body.

On the occasions of their rare meetings, Frank clutched his former lover, angrily stamped his feet when separating, and

howled with pain. During our sessions he kept painfully revisit-
ing his one great error: to have left her! He would have liked to
change the course of events. His universe was totally discon-
nected from reality; he moved through an imaginary world. My
interpretation couldn't stop there, however. What was this chaos
of anxiety and terror underneath his imaginary universe? That
was the issue that needed further investigation.

THE DEAD ENDS OF TRANSFERENCE

If Frank believed his loved one held his life in her hands, if he
was totally impotent before her power, I wagered that there was
some sort of truth to be found there. Induced by the presence
of another man at her side, the all-powerfulness of this ex-lover
reduced him to a defenseless object. He imagined that she, or
even the inseparable couple she formed with his rival, possessed
a tyrannical desire to make him suffer. Frank had no idea what
caused this despotic feeling. Yet he wasn't lying about his suffering: he felt abandoned in a meaningless world and if he tirelessly repeated the same things, it was because his turmoil gave
him a sense of existing—of being alive.

The sessions that I had with Frank didn't escape this tyranny.
My slightest observation had the weight of a distressing verdict,
as much for me as for him. Each and every word took on terrifying importance, because in his eyes I was a powerful goddess
dispensing life and death. In those moments, the transference
became as hard for me as for him. Frank awaited a miracle from
these sessions: the definitive, durable return of the loved one,
which he believed to be indispensable to his life. I searched, in
the narrow interstices that remained open to me, for paths that
would allow Frank to access a pain that worked in silence to
endanger all his relationships.

Because the pain had never been shared with anyone before, the experience that plunged Frank into his solitude hadn't yet been realized as a real affliction; it had not, strictly speaking, been truly lived—it remained suspended, outside of time. However, no matter how much he rifled through, scrutinized, and tried to get close to his feelings, he couldn't. Having missed in his life a trusted witness with whom he could share his pain, Frank didn't know how to talk to me, nor did he know how to create with me an intimate space where he could feel heard at the very place where he was hurting. My job therefore was to try to find in what he was saying something that could be linked to the real origins of his jealousy.

"I AM A HANDSOME GUY"

One day Frank described to me how he waited attentively for a sign of love from his former girlfriend. I asked him to tell me what thoughts were passing through his mind. As if trying to ward off a curse, he surprised himself by saying out loud: "I am handsome, I am handsome."

A child feels ugly when he feels neglected, no longer enveloped in his mother's loving embrace. Finally the traces of what Frank had missed were emerging: his mother's gaze—without which every small child feels destitute. In talking to himself out loud, he was addressing the distraught child inside. In saying "I am handsome, I am handsome," Frank gave us access to the ugly wretchedness into which he had sunk. The interrupted narrative of an absent history could thus begin. The rival, the loser who was so ugly, in fact, resembled him like a brother—a fallen brother.

Frank seemed to repeat this mantra, "I am handsome," in order to give himself courage in combat. It wasn't a triumphant mantra; it was not an expression of that self-complacency he had pointedly demonstrated for so long. I suggested to him that through these words he was returning to a face he must have lost when his mother's gaze turned away from him—in all likelihood at the death of his mother's sister, which happened when he was three years old. The two women were very close, nearly twins, and the car accident that had killed the sister had been painfully felt by Frank's young mother. For a long time she had been ill because of it, refusing to feed herself at a time when the child's father was away because of work. Having been left suspended for so long, the agony of Frank's collapse could at last be expressed, and his memories started to flow again. In the depths of his jealousy, did he not say that he felt as though sucked under the wheels of a car, just as had happened to his mother's adored sister? He had never made the connection before.

Frank was moved by the evocation of this lost face being linked to his mother's mourning. His memories flooded back, particularly those about his mother's illness, a time when she could no longer get up or move and remained immobile for long hours with her child at her side. Rigid like a dead person? Indeed, and Frank used to bustle about trying to wake her until, discouraged, he would sit down to wait. Through the words we exchanged, he recovered the right to have a face again.

Words restore a space for unidentified anxiety. In this case they allowed Frank to address anew the sensation of being adrift that he had felt when faced with the collapse of his mother and that had, until now, remained enigmatic and elusive. No doubt it was the same depressed look he had shown me the day his jealousy erupted that he had seen in his mother the day after the death of her sister.

THE TEMPTATION OF ANOREXIA

A forgotten breakdown, an uncommunicated pain, had left a breach in the fabric of Frank's memory. Jealousy then served as a placeholder, giving shape and meaning. His own ugliness as a neglected child was reflected in the image of his rival, as an echo of the shattered halo of beauty that had estranged him from himself. Our conversation returned the words to a pain that had gone astray. Jealousy didn't provide Frank with anything but an unsubstantial outline. It disoriented and exhausted him with vain agonies. With the invocation "I am handsome" repeated ad nauseam, Frank tried to relive the time when he and his mother had been enveloped in beauty. One can easily imagine that at such a tender age he would have wanted to return to a time when he experienced an even tighter bond with his mother, going so far as to lose weight in order to share the ethereal image of the deceased sister, and thus find himself beneath the same wheels.

When I questioned him about losing weight, Frank revealed that his mother had told him that several months after the death of his aunt, he went through quite a serious period of anorexia. Feeling weightless during his fits of jealousy evoked memories of when he had thought he must not weigh on his mother; he had looked after her instead of demanding that she pay attention to him. She abandoned herself to wait for death, rejecting all desire to live without her sister. Called on to occupy the impossible place of a dead person, the child was no longer himself. Searching to understand these confusions, he had allowed himself to believe that his mother could no longer cope with the small boy. His jealousy revived the pain of having sacrificed his sexual identity to form one body with his mother. No longer a beautiful boy adored by his mother, he had become weightless—with no needs or appetite. When the child's sensual appetite remains unquenched, the torment increases, leaving somatic sensations as the only means of expressing this psychological distress: floating, drifting, being sucked under, feeling weightless. "Who is this all for?" I had to ask myself. Where was this other who, through her failing, left the subject unconnected? Could I become a listener for him to break his solitude?

Encountering Frank face to face (instead of when he was lying on the couch) and making these connections at a time when he was feeling most destitute, finally freed him. At last he had found a witness who was not lost in nostalgia and depression. Jealousy was no longer his only recourse. Frank grabbed hold of my words like he would a lifejacket. The scene of his absence from himself began to exist. The pain unlived had reintegrated into his original body, and he felt for the first time liberated from his present stage of jealousy.

Thanks to analysis, Frank discovered that as a young boy he had nearly sunk into a meaningless world. He had all but left his body through the anorexia that made him so light. Later on, jealousy came to replace the chasm that he had hoped to avoid by breaking it off with his girlfriend before she left him. Through his jealousy Frank fell into a world of imaginary loves, where his exasperation with all the excitement made it difficult for him to form strong attachments.

THE NOSTALGIC TEMPTATION OF THE RETURN

For Frank, the artificial worlds of jealousy were attractive, as were the wheels of the car under which he felt himself being sucked in the deepest moments of his distress. The jealousy that appeared during the course of his analysis had at least revealed the collapse he had carefully masked by living a false life as a sexual adult—engaging himself in female conquests. Soon, however, it began to frighten Frank that he could feel so detached from his former lover, and he wanted to return to the previous state of jealousy which, while it had painfully bothered him, had also protected him from any encounter with his childhood. He who does not face up to things cannot rebuild himself.

A psychoanalyst encounters her patient's suffering using her own experience of pain, with the paths that she has found to pull herself through, and with the memories she keeps of the ordeals. If, however, she truly wants to help her patients, she must fight against the forces that drag them backward. I had to put our work on the line when Frank, almost to the point of rage, announced that he wanted to destroy all our recent hard-won insights and return to the jealousy he so enjoyed. If he wanted to follow that path it would have to be without me.

Through a dream, Frank showed me that he had understood my message. "I am on a highway and I arrive at a fork in the road. On one road, there is a toll, one often has to stop, and there is a risk of accidents. On the other road, a vehicle awaits me, a sort of rocket in which I recognize all my fears represented by different objects—it wants to take me up to the skies." The rocket of excitement and jealousy represented a false hope, instead of a real desire that has an awareness of the possible accidents on the route of life. Frank finally chose to no longer bypass the obstacles and continue his route along the road of the tolls and forced stops—that of real life (and of his analysis!). He could therefore now try to encounter and construct a relationship that was not inhabited only by the passionate excitement caused by jealousy.

CHAPTER 4

CAROL: RESTORING SELF-ESTEEM THROUGH JEALOUSY

arol couldn't keep still in her sessions with me. Her arms and legs twitched nervously in jerking motions. At the age of thirty, a scientific researcher by trade with a rather flustered appearance, she was at once beautiful and childlike. To remain seated seemed to take superhuman effort and she chattered away without taking a breath. According to her account, her life had been one long failure, professionally and emotionally, and her previous analyses too. Despite her higher education, she remained in a precarious social position, both emotionally and financially, and although she had had sexual relationships very early, they had been rare and unhappy.

The last relationship summarized them all: Carol was involved with a man who seemed to show her extreme indifference, a man she rarely saw. She pursued this almost nonexistent relationship for several years without managing to let go. She would sharply reproach him for having relationships with other women, and described herself as obsessed by this man's presumed desire to make her jealous.

With great difficulty, because she talked about him with a passion that could have made one believe there was an intense, reciprocated romance, I managed to grasp that the alliance with this man had briefly existed sometime in the past, but that it was presently very sporadic. This relationship seemed to be invented with the sole aim of allowing her jealousy to feed her suffering, which illustrated perfectly Freud's theory of feminine masochism. According to Freud, feminine masochism is a woman's destiny. In other words, a woman, by nature, waits indefinitely inside the home of the man while he, by nature flighty, is all the more envied because he is occupied and drawn to the outside world. Such a woman believes herself to be faceless and is consumed by her envy of other women who are unknown to her, yet imbued with erotic powers she doesn't possess. These other women are imagined as remarkable and attractive, while she is not.

Carol put a great amount of energy into making herself unhappy and knew, to perfection, how to torture herself. When I asked her what attracted her to her lover, she didn't have any clear answer. Whenever they left each other, she could not tear herself away and pursued him with telephone calls, accused him of deceiving her, and screamed of her jealousy. In these moments she behaved, she said, like a harpy and hated herself for acting this way. At least in this case, her jealousy was not contained, or interior, or reduced to silence. However, she was incapable of controlling this humiliating behavior that only intensified her former lover's exasperation and disdain. She wanted me to help her put an end to this jealousy.

REDISCOVERING THE KEYS OF HER INNER HOME

The first year of Carol's analysis was dominated by her stories about this man. She arrived at sessions dishevelled and in a frenzy, and twisted herself on the couch with rage over the fact that this man neglected her for other women. Stuck on him, she refused to talk about anything else, and I felt her hysteria escalate during the course of one particular session. When it reached its peak, Carol demanded that I obtain for her "simply that thing that all women have," without being any more precise. "I want it, and that's all!" she proclaimed. What was she asking for? I had no idea. She seemed to think that my other patients had all received something from me that she herself wasn't getting. I felt powerless to help her. Furthermore, she spent the better part of her time formulating unscrupulous plans to discredit her former lover and to get her revenge.

Overwhelmed by her talk, I chose instead to be guided by what I felt in her presence. Our sessions were invaded by what was happening outside of them, and in her eyes, the space we shared did not exist. I felt negated. One day she provided a morsel of information that was the trigger for a turning point. As she often forgot to lock her apartment door, she found herself frequently robbed of various objects. I suggested to her that her own interior was represented symbolically by her apartment: she did nothing to protect her privacy, as everyone and anyone was allowed to enter her space.

For the first time, I had the impression that she was really listening to me. She became aware of the fact that her behavior produced an effect and that she had the means to act in order to stop being a victim. She was amazed. She realized she had a private side. She was split between delighted surprise and a resolve to prove to me that privacy wasn't her thing.

She began, however, to protect her home. Allowing herself to shut the door on distant acquaintances, she forbade them from stopping by whenever they liked. The nature of her presence in our sessions changed also. She was able to understand finally why she let herself be ravaged, as if under an injunction to be a victim, at the mercy of others' whims.

The space of her home, exposed to all insults and abuse, was a ravaged place. Her apartment was a metaphor for her self: a nonspace. By acknowledging that she too had a right to privacy, I permitted her to reinvest in a feminine interior that was truly her own. The day she finally decided to lock her apartment door, she erected an effective barrier against the destructive pleasure of being nothing. Being able to enclose her space of privacy, she thus affirmed that it held a certain value for her; it was no longer nothing. My remarks were really addressed to her body, which was represented by her apartment; these words authorized her to let this nonspace become a real place.

That changed nothing, however, in how she interacted with her former lover. "I am fighting to not think about him all the time, but I can't stop myself from imagining that he wants to get rid of me so he can be with someone else, and this makes me want to throw myself at him. I'm really addicted to jealousy." It was completely useless to point out the imaginary dimension of their bond. She would have fought me tooth and nail to protect the power she granted her lover. She needed the excitement of jealousy to make her suffer all the more.

THE POISONED TUNIC OF JEALOUSY

Carol was a woman in love, without a doubt. But, above all, she was possessed by an overpowering male image. Her lover provoked in her a feeling of uselessness and jealousy. This authority he had over her, invented by her obsessive overattention, was both terrifying and exciting. She was an addict of jealousy, capable of cultivating unlimited amounts of her own drug! Carol valued no other discussion than the repeated description of the excesses to which her jealousy drove her. She seemed rooted in a painful and humiliating limbo.

I believed that Carol found refuge in her jealousy as one might wrap oneself in a second skin. Perhaps the memory of her difficulty in separating from her lover made me resort to this image of a skin. In fact, at the time of leaving him, after their rare encounters, it was like he "stole her skin," she said. "We are of the same pelt and we rip it to shreds," she added. In the worst fits of her jealousy, she suffered so terribly that it was as if she had been "skinned alive."

To a certain extent, by giving rise to this suffering, her jealousy offered a solution to her fear of being nothing. "Better a painful skin than none at all," whispered her jealousy.

The fantasy that certain masochists have to form one skin with their mother can be attributed to their inability to grow up, to build a barrier that would allow pleasure and pain to be regulated. In the best of circumstances, this encounter allows the child to build an erogenous image of her body. Her "pelt" is as much a true skin, a skin caressed by words and the proximity to another body, as a skin barrier between the child and the conscious and unconscious emotions of her mother. The masochist, on the other hand, experiences her sense of self, not as separate from the mother's but as dangerously close to the mother's whims. The masochist dulls her anxiety by inventing a second skin that binds her closer to the torturer-mother rather than serving as a barrier between them. This strategy affords her the illusion that she is at least in control of the pain she inflicts upon herself.

If Carol found refuge in the second skin of her masochistic behavior, the excitement of her jealousy brought her back to a primordial suffering: the tearing of the pelt that had been formed by her mother's lack of attention to her body and her being. Carol's way of fighting against menace was to get intoxicated with fury and rage while clutching her lover. She appeared to be unable to fully exist except in these moments of jealous excitement. She was indifferent to everything else.

Eventually, though, a breach opened in the wall of her lamentations. The man she "love-hated" was atypically friendly one day. Despite that, Carol indulged in one of her crises of jealousy. The fit deterred and once again distanced her lover. Although she blamed herself for it, she was hysterical with rage and anger toward him. I asked during one of our sessions: "But finally how do you want him to treat you? When he's nice and full of kindness, that's not right! Yet if he rejects you, that really makes you angry!" And I added, "Who is this repelling figure who, despite everything, you seek at all costs?" She conceded: "When I was with him, I thought about my father, of the hatred I have for him. My mother has remained very attached to him despite everything he has done. I certainly haven't. One could say she remains attached to him by a thread. I don't want to be faithful to her . . . she betrayed me." I replied, "She betrayed you with your father, she abandoned you to him?" She responded, "Yes, oh yes! She accepted everything from my father. She let him examine me from every angle under the pretext that he was a doctor!"

One thing gradually leading to another, I found out that her mother had been an accomplice in the father's incestuous enjoyment of his daughter. With his wife's approval, he had sexually abused his daughter. I now clearly understood why Carol had made her apartment and her body a nonspace. By doing so, she prevented the suffering associated with being deprived of all privacy. The odious, repelling sheepskin concealed this absence of privacy. It made Carol eternally her mother's daughter, under the weight of an oath that she could not understand. Yet to be her daughter did not grant her an existence per se. Crushed by the father's sadism, her mother was unable to show Carol how to be a woman who is not ravaged by a man. But Carol could not express any violence toward the intrusive and insulting behavior of her father, for fear of letting her mother down. She could not hate her father's incestuous violence. Carol believed she had to support her mother at all costs, which meant she could not pick and choose what she received from her. The painful rage in which she enveloped herself masked the absence of an active and free femininity; she was trapped in the prison of her mother's passivity, herself a victim, who abandoned her daughter to her husband's voyeuristic and infantile urges. Because her mother did not separate herself, for her daughter's sake, from her own masochistic enjoyment in being an object of contempt, she condemned her child to an eternal position of submission to masculine violence.

By allowing Carol to finally say, "No, I don't want to be her daughter," the analysis permitted a separation between her and the worst aspects of her mother, to whom she remained faithful despite herself. This intimate revelation allowed Carol to take a step forward. She consented to stop showing solidarity until death to her mother, preferring to show solidarity to life. At the same time, she managed to detach herself from her father's gaze, which was tainted with hatred toward her mother. If they didn't love each other, she discovered, that was their business. There was nothing forcing Carol to remain tied to them by a thread. She decided to stop playing the imbecile to protect the men who treated her badly. Playing the imbecile was being the masochistic girl, always submissive to the uncompromising will of a man. The suffering caused by her jealousy helped her maintain a fiction: men have everything, women have nothing, men are everything, and women are nothing.

THE UNINHABITED TERRITORIES OF FEMININITY

Carol wanted what all women have. She felt deprived of this mysterious feminine quality that she had asked me to give her. Her jealousy drove her to want to take from every other woman, including her analyst, something that was in her imagination. Having received nothing from her mother but distressing and terrifying mysteries regarding her sex, she had to beg for this something from a man.

Carol had to remain the passive extension of her mother, the receptacle of the hatred that bound her parents. The way in which her mother had permitted the father's enjoyment of his daughter, without respect for her privacy, had symbolically killed her and her femininity. Carol had experienced this as a bottomless betrayal. Her mother had dragged her into the same disaster as her own. Her mother had not erected a barrier strong enough to obstruct her husband's sadistic and intrusive tendencies. She had in that sense renounced the ethical function in which mothers protect their children from fathers who confuse their masculinity with infantile fantasies of all-powerfulness. Through her submissiveness, Carol's mother was unable to distinguish masculine virtues from sheer force, and was unable to offer her daughter a definition of femininity that was both pleasurable and safe. Carol had no other solution than to revert to the masochistic path. Through the jealousy that tore her apart, Carol screamed her pain in being bound to her mother by a poisoned pelt.

Not only did she cry over her mother's abandonment, but she also tried to free herself from the devalued model of a relationship, where the daughter was thrown to the lions as the prey of her parents' sadomasochistic enjoyment. Having found a man who rejected her, Carol reenacted with him the drama that defined her childhood. She screamed to me of how her skin was "irritated and scorched." It would be wrong to call Carol a masochist who enjoyed the pain she endured. She was in a sense much more of a fighter than her mother, who accepted the abuse of her husband and his use of her daughter. Carol ardently searched for recognition, for a knife that could cut the umbilical cord, and for a father figure whose masculine presence would not trigger hate and contempt, but respect and pleasure for her budding femininity.

INDIFFERENCE AND VIOLENCE

The indifference that parents sometimes manifest toward their children is much more harmful than it at first appears. Their withdrawal is a convenient form of resentment. Yet children like Carol can't understand why they become the victims of this silent rage that is passed from generation to generation. As varied as it may be, parents or grandparents have no inkling that this rage deflates their children's appetite to live and love. The message they received growing up—that femininity and masculinity are synonyms of submission and violence—are passed on to their children. As a response, the new generation fights back using whatever tactics they can to reinvent hope even if it comes at the cost of immense suffering.

The way in which a mother connects to her own femininity and how she allows her daughter to partake in its pleasures while still enabling her to separate in order to assume her own existence is at the heart of a girl's development.

FICTIONALIZING THE PAIN OF BEING NOTHING

As humans we have the ability, through language, to transform our reality into a fiction that is no longer related to the actual suffering. Making a pain unreal is to evade it—behavior common to every human being. Different from negation, which purely and simply denies the conflict, fictionalization is a process that allows it to escape elsewhere, making it elusive. Through her masochistic scenarios, which both denied and denounced her parents, Carol projected her difficulty onto a fictionalized reality where her experience at being nothing became unreal. Sartre describes this experience when he compares it to drinking sea water to quench one's thirst. "It is not that I deny my thirst, rather I drink something that resembles water, but what I drink is a water that is unreal and does not quench my thirst." In other words, Carol displayed the tenets of a pain that both revealed and refuted her existence as a victim of abuse.

At least Carol's jealousy pulled her into a more active role. She shouted her desire to exist, her craving to be recognized, and her hatred for her parents who kept her in this vacuum where she struggled to find the meaning of love. But this led her into a vicious cycle in which her rage was fed by a feeling of worthlessness. Unable to unearth the original pain that caused her predicament, she kept trying, with the wrong tools, to cut an acute pain off at the root.

When, thanks to her analysis, Carol consented to take a step forward, the influence of her parents' alliance fell to pieces. Her jealousy, through the excitement it generated, kept in limbo her anguish at being nothing. Carol's jealousy was her only path to gaining access to real emotions, even if it only backfired in not providing her with either the tools to separate from her mother or the ability to find expression for the hatred she felt toward her father. Carol remained stuck, so to speak, to her mother's pathetic vision of femininity. From that place, it was impossible for her to experience the original pain that had determined her predicament: that of being abandoned with no one to turn to.

"What gave me confidence in you," she told me later, "was that I didn't manage to seduce you; so I could therefore go all the way. I knew you would survive!" Carol needed to know that, unlike her mother, I could survive her anger and be there for her despite her jealous fits and her self-destructive behavior.

In showing her that her passionately jealous conduct was her attempt at substituting one pain for another, she was finally able to retrieve her original suffering. After that, her masochistic behavior disappeared and with that her jealousy.

If the analyst wants to help a woman like Carol, she is driven to imagine these places where nothing feels as though it really exists. Imagining means leaving oneself behind in order to travel toward the other. The here and now where such a patient calls me to meet her is a place where I must think like a geographer. The space of the here and now shows me the flaws in her attempts to make sense of the past where pain could find no words or emotions to give it life. The analyst then becomes an explorer of unknown lands, where she must voyage in a "jealous" boat and is never sure of arriving on land intact.

CHAPTER 5

BROTHERS AND SISTERS:
ONE'S EARLIEST ENCOUNTERS WITH JEALOUSY

The bonds one has with brothers and sisters are part and parcel of how we define ourselves. If a child has no sibling, she chooses one of her friends to fill the role. Adolescents confront authority more willingly (since their family falls into the background) when they are part of a gang of friends that imitate each other. With friends, an adolescent can recognize himself. Similarly, when children are with others their own age who are more resourceful than they are, their motor skill development increases dramatically.

The jealousy between brothers and sisters reveals a vulnerability that threatens to be awakened in anyone. "What more does he/she have than I do?" wonders a brother or sister. Jealousy between siblings therefore clarifies jealousy's essential motives and even in some cases its origin. Jealousy exposes the anxiety a person faces when kicked out of a place that he or she thought was their own. It blows the foundations of identity to pieces especially when they are unstable or in formation. It exposes the fragility of the boundaries between self and other, and shows the individual how precarious the limits of the self can be. The little boy or girl can fall apart. The same process is at work in adult jealousy. In other words, when an adult is in the grip of jealousy, it is safe to assume that this always refers to an identity crisis in childhood. Rivalry between brothers and sisters may be painful but it is also comforting. It affords a measure of comparison and identification that fortifies the child's sense of self. He learns through this process to be both similar and different from his rival. It is important therefore to understand what mental processes are involved when a child attempts to imagine who he is, and therefore how he compares with his siblings.

The child who hasn't yet constructed a solid identity is less convinced than the adult of what he is and what he represents. If he does not yet speak, he is all the more prey to jealousy. Language permits us to hear ourselves think, to step back and look upon ourselves from the outside. The child who speaks is more confident of his capabilities and therefore better able to understand himself. Language, in this case, may help defuse the effects of jealousy. As the child can tell himself a story about who he is, he is more equipped to fend off the threat posed by another, both like himself and other than himself.

But, even so, some work is needed to overcome an attack of jealousy. A very young child does not yet have an adequate supply of emotional experience or achievement to assure that he can survive this type of challenge.

Take one young woman I saw for a while: during her attacks of jealousy, she had to repeat to herself a list of all her achievements in order to once again feel whole! This recapitulation gave her back a face and a body, which jealousy had taken away.

The more anchored one is in reality, the shorter the time it takes to recall oneself, which gives jealousy less of an opportunity to solidify in the form of a trauma. Jealousy, like an X-ray, reveals the absence of foundations, over which the construction of an identity wavers. If a child has not received clear and loving indications of her place in the family constellation, she is more likely to develop jealous tendencies.

Is it so surprising that classic descriptions of jealousy are focused on the young child who bitterly contemplates a new arrival in the family? There the child openly demonstrates what the jealous adult denies when in the throes of a love affair: the inability to distinguish between himself and another.

Jealousy toward someone younger than oneself

Let's consider the jealousy suffered by a child who is very small, almost a baby, and hasn't yet learned to speak. The child, fascinated by the image of its mother breastfeeding another child, is filled with rage. All of jealousy's future blows derive from this first clash with a rival. Whether the jealous person's doubts slowly worm their way into him or thunder down like a ton of bricks, the arrival of jealousy always designates a before and an after. "Nothing is as it used to be," say jealous men and women. The day of their lost serenity remains forever marked as a red-letter day.

Let's look at this first shock of jealousy in another way. The small child imitates those who love him and speak to him. He develops fantasies that bring together his bodily experiences and his desire to live. In the process of freeing himself from his condition as a baby, one such fantasy that the child has is to grow up. Yet this fantasy is in sharp contrast to the baby's biological reality. He can't reach what he envies. The child who cannot speak does not yet possess a stable representation of his interior space, or a trustworthy map of the frontiers that separate him from those who surround him. He is exposed to the terror of being alone with no way out. The younger he is, the more his defensive tactics appear to be a double-edged sword, isolating him further from the outside world.

What is the nature of the trauma that occurs in this tiny child? The child is jealous, not of an object (the breast) that had been taken away from him, but of the relationship he perceives between two beings. This moment of collapse happens again in all the adult circumstances that trigger jealousy.

The child, not yet entirely developed, who doesn't yet know how to talk, has a tendency to confuse himself with the baby he sees in his mother's arms. At the same time, his maturity means that he possesses more autonomy than the infant he bitterly observes. Drawn one way by the image he sees, and the other by his desire to be grown up and autonomous, the child no longer knows who he is or who he should try to be. His mother's desire becomes a mystery to him. He no longer understands what she wants from him or what she loves, and he suffers because of the baby. His mother appears to him to be other than the person he used to know who enveloped him in her attentions. Sometimes she may even seem ugly to him. At this moment the child perceives that his mother has an enigmatic interior that conflicts with the beautiful harmony he wishes to share with her.

A dangerous confusion builds in him. His status as an individual collapses at the very moment he's just grabbed hold of it. The child, now plagued with jealousy, is no longer able to distinguish between the benefits of love and the advantages of his destructive impulses. Love permitted him to identify with the good things he received and to grow up. His destructive impulses have opened a path of detachment for him. If the child can imagine that he has the power to destroy the bond to his mother, he can then freely enjoy the permanence of this loving caretaker, who will survive the destructive wishes of the child. It is only then that a loved one can be placed outside the zone of all-powerful thoughts which, in the first stages of existence, give the illusion that reality conforms to one's desires. In other words, there is no difference between fantasy and reality in the child's mind. The oscillation between love and destructivity that is necessary to mental life and to the clarification of what is real and what isn't is left pending when jealousy is aroused. The jealous child no longer knows where to go. He is stationary. Jealousy causes a stalemate between love and the wish to break free from his mother.

Solitude

Whether the child encounters or imagines someone younger or someone the same age, the child becomes aware of what he has lost (his mother) and also, the solitude attached to this loss. The young child experiences the presence of his self at the very moment when he feels displaced from his mother. This time is all the more delicate if the child has only just begun to tear himself away from his fantasies of fusion with his mother, where he gave himself the necessary illusion of *already being grown up*. At the moment when he *sees* himself in someone other to him, his mother also appears other, foreign, unknown, enigmatic, and far off. The child, in the traumatic confrontation with someone like him (that could even be him), realizes he is an individual, different from every other person. From then on every time the likelihood of losing an important position appears, the risk of jealousy will inevitably be there too.

The intensity of this jealousy has serious consequences for mental functioning. The ability to endure uncertainties, to be open to an unknown future, is undermined by the anxiety that mobilizes jealousy. Rigid, the jealous person is all the more so when he does not find himself loveable. For the child, the only way out is his resilience, his wish to live, his fantasies of what can make him happy.

The child wants to grow up, to separate himself from those who at one time carried him, and to head toward the unknown. But he is prevented from doing so by the traumatic experience of jealousy. This temporary impasse can go unnoticed. The child is then driven to imitate the person who attracts his mother's or father's attention. He thus returns to a stage in development that he had already passed and this regression is painful. For example, a child already weaned takes the bottle just like a baby. Behind this action the child effectively shows that he has lost sight of his pride in being a big boy. It is better to go along with the behavior (by making light of it, for instance), to accompany him rather than frustrate him. By enjoying this stage of regression we let the child play around with it instead of worsening the situation.

OLDER AND YOUNGER SIBLINGS

It isn't unusual to hear a child, jealous of the birth of a younger sibling, say "we'll send him back" or "let her go back to where she came from." A young girl might say in front of her brother, "Do you think he's really worth that much?" No one likes to lose his bearings, and the new arrival, although loved, remains an intruder. When one envies another, he alienates himself *to* the one he envies. This scrambling of oneself and another is one of the many characteristics of jealousy.

Children go through times of regression when they are jealous, but they can get out of them, provided the solution isn't hindered by the unconscious conflicts of their parents. If the child is fragile, his parents' ambivalence will impair his wish to grow up and to differentiate himself from them. His jealousy will become the sign of his inability to find his proper place. One child, separated from his family for some time due to his mother's ill health, returned to find himself inflicted with the epithet "jeal-ous" every time he got angry with those who had stayed home. Misunderstood, this child became the jealous one in the fam-ily, and his ability to sort out his place among his brothers and sisters was therefore frozen in its tracks.

If ever the child, in battle with himself, discovers either a willed or involuntary sign of denial of his efforts by another, his mental development is hindered. The effects of these rejections are all the worse if they are addressed to a very young child, who is still connected to the world of his mother's emotions. He will scrutinize her all the more frantically, searching for signs of her desire. The child questions, "Is there or is there not something valid and meaningful in her love?"

The smaller the child, the more his wait is filled with anxiety, and the more the words he receives are precious. If his mother seems to prefer another child, the separation between the two of them will feel like a death. "I've always wanted to have a daugh-ter," one mother might say, without thinking, to her small son who is sick with jealousy since the birth of his small sister. No longer occupying a special place in his mother's life, no longer feeling supported, he wonders why he should grow up, and he passes through a period of depression. This situation conceals another one that is all the more radical: a child needs to know for *whom* to grow up. When the answer to this question makes no sense, the child can fail to mature.

It has become common currency to talk about jealousy be-tween older and younger siblings. Certain parents tolerate such demonstrations of intense jealousy without perceiving that these demonstrations are addressed to them; however, their refusal or inability to intervene, because they think that jealousy among siblings is normal, is worrisome for both the child who violently expresses his jealousy and for the one who endures it. In both cases, the space of the child's inner world is invaded by his parents' own conflicts and impasses.

RIVALRY AND IMITATION

The younger child admires the elder for his status as big, and for the simple fact that he has preceded the younger one in life. The younger one seeks to resemble him and, at the same time, would like to distinguish himself from his brother. Jealous of the privileges of the elder, the younger one acts out more openly. Jealousy teaches him to learn to differ. However, such jealousy toward an elder sibling is far less troublesome when acted upon. Otherwise the child runs the risk of jealousy remaining masked and invisible for a long time before manifesting itself in a catastrophic way.

Whereas the rivalry toward an older sibling leads to a conflict between the desire to resemble him and the desire to distinguish oneself from him, in a more regressive phase, the younger child merely imitates the elder. The child imprisoned in this way hates the elder as a way of expelling this burden to imitate.

Certain delirious states of mind and the majority of cases of anorexia tend to begin in adolescence. When we look for an element that might have caused these problems, it is common to find that a dearly loved brother or sister has either left home or begun an amorous liaison only a short time before the eruption of trouble. Intense jealousy often accompanies these problems. The jealousy is all the more alienating if the child's identity is based on imitating a brother or sister.

One such young girl became anorexic after her older sister did. "I had a shock seeing her so skinny," she told me. "My sister no longer thought about me, but about food, and she was happy!" During one of our sessions the girl later added, "I have stopped eating too to show my sister my body so that she might finally see herself as she is. I want her to go back to how she was." This young girl had lived in the fantasy of a common body between herself and her sister; in a certain manner, she had shared her identity. Also, when this younger sister, for reasons of her own, had begun her hunger strike, she was distraught to learn that she was no longer one with her older sister. She learned of the existence of a rival: anorexia. She began to live through it, by wanting to be *like* the anorexia of her sister.

At one extreme, this kind of jealousy demonstrates the desire for domination that all jealous individuals have. Anorexics no longer see themselves in the gaze of others and are pleased with this unreal image of their body. The situation of this young girl shows us how much she wanted to reflect the *image* of her sister. By not being able to stabilize an internal image of her own body, she borrowed from her sister.

If every jealous person suffers from an inability to distinguish (temporarily or long-term) between herself and another, it is not surprising to acknowledge that the persistence of the one (confusion) leads to the permanence of the other (jealousy).

THE FLUCTUATIONS OF THE JEALOUS INDIVIDUAL

Jealousy is not only normal but it is a necessary emotion for a child growing up. If a child is shielded from the experience of jealousy, he won't be able to handle competition and envy as an adult and may as a result be seriously stifled both in his relationships and professional ambitions. Jealousy forces children to test the limits of who they are when they are forced to compare themselves to their siblings. A younger sibling may be jealous of the privileges of his older brother and sister, but at the same time he can realize what he can aspire to while still enjoying the attention and care of his parents. An older sibling can envy the baby in the family who gets his way without being scolded, but he can also be proud of his independence. Jealousy in that sense helps to delineate the space that is his, and differentiates him from others. The wavering between wanting to be like the other and yet coming to grips with who he is, is a necessary part of growing up.

But jealousy can be more threatening when it becomes fixed. When a child feels excluded from the attention of his parents or rejected by his siblings, in order to fend off the feeling of having no place of his own, he will revert to imitation. He will want to be the other, do what the other does, copy his behavior rather than find ways to distinguish himself and become his own person.

As much as a child has a need to imitate his older siblings and his peers with the aim of testing his limits, sharing his experiences, and discovering what is truly his own, he may also revert to the alienating strategies of pure imitation if he is not given his proper place among his brothers and sisters.

Jealousy plays a crucial role in human development when a child is confronted with the mysteries of sexual difference. What does it mean to be a boy or a girl? Such gender positions are not fixed but depend on the meaning that the parents attribute to them. A mother may favor her daughter over her son, or the father may favor the son. As a result, the child's feeling of pride or shame, of belonging to one gender or another, will trigger questions and anxieties such as "What does she or he have that I don't? What is my rival really worth?" It's difficult to learn to love one's gender when one gets mixed messages growing up. But it's even more challenging to grasp what the other sex represents. The meaning of the other sex is revealed through the trial between siblings. The relationship permits the child to explore the floating masculine and feminine positions of his brothers and sisters. Indeed these positions are not set in stone and have flexible meanings according to the ways fathers and mothers perceive the roles and attributes of their sons and daughters. When jealousy hits, it is possible to grapple with and enjoy the rewards of sexual difference between brothers and sisters that are ordinarily kept hidden. For it is otherness, sexual or otherwise, that triggers jealousy. To imagine that one is excluded from something that the other receives is always linked to the mysteries of sex and love. This is especially true for those who were not able to confront their jealous impulses growing up.

It is not surprising therefore that when we encounter the ferocity of jealousy in amorous relationships we are often brought back to the intensity of sibling rivalries. A man will be all the more jealous of another if he resembles his brother, or a woman if another resembles her sister. Unfinished business of the past comes back with a vengeance when one's sense of identity as a lovable man or woman has not been sufficiently elaborated in childhood. Under these circumstances, a rival who is too close for comfort can evoke in the jealous individual the terrifying feeling of being displaced to the point of psychic death, reawakening in the adult the terror of the time when imitation of a sibling shielded the experience of blurred boundaries between self and other. This is why it is so important for children to be given the space and security to openly experience sibling rivalry during childhood. To do so dispels later in life the horrible suffering caused by the presence of a rival, real or imagined.

CHAPTER 6

DAVID: A MAN WITHOUT JEALOUSY

J ealousy was a sentiment completely alien to David—he was not the type of man to be jealous. "Is it a feeling that one must experience in order to be normal?" he asked me, his words laced with irony. "Do you consider that relationships are loving only when they are marked by this sort of possessiveness?"

With a discreet smile of jubilation, he informed me that he and his wife had an open marriage. They had set up an arrangement of reciprocal generosity: each would lead his or her own erotic life, because "life is long and it would be pointless to deprive each other of the encounters it has to offer," he remarked. Ordinarily, one hears: "Life is so short, that one must seize every opportunity." It surprised me that David found life so incredibly long.

David was a fifty-year-old lawyer who had come to me because, he said, he had lost all joy in his life. A sort of inexpressible fatigue seemed to emanate from his large, heavy body. Behind his amiable stance as a man who was never jealous, I felt a sense of apathy and disgust that went much deeper than his demeanor suggested. He owed it to himself to make every woman happy—his own partner, of course, but also those he spent time with, his female friends as well as his mistresses. His favorite occupation was to encourage their encounters with other men. Yet he did not display an ounce of jealousy. On the contrary, he advertised a satisfaction that left me bemused.

Every man is free to lead his life as he wishes. It is not up to psychoanalysts to determine the sex, number, or choice of partners of their patients. All therapists stand somewhat alone and destitute in the face of the mysteries of sexuality. It would be useless to advocate a hierarchy of sexual discoveries, as they all lead to the same place: toward a repair of secret wounds.

So, what was it that bothered me about David? What evil lurked in wanting to make women, both friends and lovers, happy? This man seemed to play with me too, trying to speak to the woman in me. He had never thought of talking to a male psychoanalyst. "Certainly not!" he exclaimed. He invited me to contemplate his dreams, which were supposed to enchant me. They were, I told myself, not something that would inspire disgust or indignation. But as I went on listening to him, my thoughts and powers of association progressively weakened. Although it was the first time we had met, there was an ease, facility, and even familiarity with which he spoke to me, which added to my discomfort.

I remained incredulous. I searched inside myself for what it was that made me feel uncomfortable with this man who seemed so preoccupied with caring for the well-being of others.

"You don't seem to like women as much as I do," he said to me in an amused and slightly condescending tone of voice. He then went off on a lengthy monologue about women and what he called femininity, which he had a vital need for, since his male relationships were of scarce interest to him. "Women," "the feminine," and "femininity" (he used all three terms indiscriminately) were, for him, the salt of life. Close to their world, he understood women better than they understood themselves. He liked to be their friend and confidant.

Was I, in his eyes, a woman like all these others? Underneath his words, I wondered if he wanted to gratify me too. Or was he possibly trying to make me understand how much I stood outside the category of women? Arguing with him inside my head, I realized he had succeeded in making me lose sight of the reasons that had brought him to visit a psychoanalyst in the first place. He said he had lost joy in life, but he didn't seem to show it. I wondered where he hoped to take his therapy.

As if reading my mind, David returned to what had brought him to me. For some time, a worrisome feeling of vagueness and anxiety had colored his encounters with women. He was alarmed that he might no longer be able to satisfy them. "Life doesn't seem to be worth living anymore," he added to complete the portrait of his depression. Moreover, having lost all interest in sex, he regarded his penis with a worrying perplexity as if he didn't know "what he had down there." Like one might erase an embarrassing blemish on someone's photograph, he distressfully acknowledged an absence concerning his sexuality. Questioning himself about women and their desires, he feared that they might want something from him that he could no longer provide. At this point he interrupted himself to ask me, "Am I boring you with my issues?"

By asking me that question and therefore exposing his anxiety about boring me, David finally revealed that a connection between us had been established. Now liberated from his hypnotic and suave generosity, I could focus on the downward slope of depression that had made him search for my help. The shackles that I felt locked into suggested to me that he longed to throw off something in which he felt confined.

I pointed out to him the constraint under which he lived: he owed it to himself to make a woman happy. Insofar as he proclaimed to have to make a woman happy, no matter which one, every stranger was liable to fill this anonymous position. He gave the impression, I added, of being burdened by an impossible task, a Sisyphean challenge. Did this have some link to the feelings he complained about of weariness, fatigue, and that life didn't seem worth living?

THE RAFT OF THE MEDUSA, OR THE SHIPWRECKS OF DESIRE

"Truly, pleasure is for other people," David said, "not for me. I've never really thought about myself much. When I make love, for example, I don't really feel anything. I don't like a woman to bother over me, to touch me; it's up to me to do it. Pleasure is always a sort of death; it is taking something away from me against my wishes." He added, laughing: "With my antidepressant pills, it's perfect. I belong to no one. I'm a real dead person. I'm also not that much fun." I thought about this dead person and the masculine frigidities that he spoke about.

After a moment of silence, he told me of the episode that had driven him to seek my help. While at the Louvre, he was looking at Géricault's painting, *The Raft of the Medusa*, which shows the terrified escapees of the eponymous frigate's shipwreck. In the middle of a raging sea, bodies, people, some surviving, some dying, are entangled, while only a few find the strength, in a last attempt, to compose themselves to call for help. As David was viewing this picture, he broke down into a violent and uncontrollable fit of tears. Submerged, from that point on, by emotions that seemed to overwhelm him, he had consulted a psychiatrist, who had been quick to prescribe him antidepressants. The drugs stopped his tears, but the feeling of vanity and lassitude that had paralyzed him remained. Destitute, he had finally decided to come and see me.

By affirming, loudly and clearly, his veneration for women, his success in relationships with them, and his absence of jealousy, did he not secretly see himself as one of the dying people in the painting? I was willing to bet on it. Perhaps it was time, I suggested to him, to return to these dying men and women the words that echoed inside him and had been neglected and silenced for too long. On hearing my words, he looked at me, intensely surprised. Visibly moved, he rediscovered the tears that had been dried up by the antidepressants. "Do you know him, this child?" he asked me, bursting into tears. A breach had opened to give him life once again.

He had made me feel the violence of the domination that strangled and extinguished his erotic desire. If David didn't have access to jealousy's arousal, was that the cause of his sexual anesthesia?

From the very beginning, David had made a point of telling me that he had just turned fifty, which was the age of his mother at the time his father left her. The father's departure left the wife furious toward men and burdened with the care of their adolescent son. The departure also hampered David by leaving him with a depressed woman. Wasn't this abandonment all the more terrifying since his father died shortly thereafter? Was the concurrence between the ages at which both David and his mother had sunk into depression coincidental? Had his mother's difficulties now begun to invade him?

A LIFELESS BODY AND A VOYEURISTIC GAZE

David then explained the nature of his relationships with women, which seemed much stranger than he had at first implied. He was the provider—cooking meals, finding them lovers, watching over everything. He made special efforts to reduce their need to do anything, so that in return they were forced to await everything from him. He provided for them financially, and his partners were rapidly transformed into poor lost girls.

I learned that he didn't satisfy himself merely with organizing rendezvous between his mistresses and their lovers, but that he liked to take part as a voyeur. However much he told himself that he wasn't excluded from their unions, seeing as it was his wish to unite male and female bodies, in his heart of hearts he only deceived himself. His desire for domination surely found satisfaction through this device, making jealousy pointless, but his success remained somewhat unreal and fantastical as it was reduced to the sole pleasure of a gaze. The satisfaction that he drew from this was slim: from the moment he offered women other lovers than himself, he forbade himself from desiring them.

"My mother told me that all men are bastards who hurt women," he said. His sexual life had been more or less developed within this context, thus combining a sense of guilt with worry. Attracted to women, he had experienced at the same time an immense terror of resembling that man his mother described. He had thus put his masculine body in brackets, contenting himself with appeasing his desires through a voyeurism from which he took only slight satisfaction. Participating at a distance in the encounter between a man and a woman, he certainly managed to short-circuit all jealousy, but his numbed body showed just how much he remained excluded from their union, deprived of the right to have an erotic body of his own. Pleasure was reserved for others. Through this way of doing things, was he not blaming his mother and father for not giving him the right to be like them, a sexual being?

Was his jealousy, in an even more radical manner, purely and simply denied in the same way as his masculinity? Did he not search to avoid, at all costs, a very painful issue: that of being a man?

MATERNAL HUMILIATION AND BRIDLED VIRILITY

On entering my office, David always stood back to let me go first. When I asked him about this habit, he replied that he preferred to remain behind me, sheltered from my gaze. I perceived that this feigned courtesy permitted him to keep me at a distance by preventing me from staring at him. "What is it that I shouldn't see?" I asked. "My body, my penis, all that," he said. He avoided showing himself nude to a woman because he thought she would be disgusted by what she saw.

"How ugly it is!" exclaimed his mother on seeing him at birth. What would she have seen if not her son's penis? He had been ashamed all his life of being a boy. The ugliness that his mother ostentatiously affirmed was also a means of alienating him from her. She didn't like this masculinity that escaped her power. A mother doesn't look at her child's sex purely with her eyes. She regards it with her love, as well as with her anxieties. Virility, for this woman, had to be negated and reduced to a vulgar morsel of flesh—a little penis that dared to raise itself, at its own command when, for example, her son accompanied her to the dressmaker. It seemed to infuriate her, and on occasion she would scream incomprehensible accusations at David that had filled him with shame.

Some time later in one of our sessions, David realized that I was not particularly disturbed by his great heavy body, so much larger than my own. He admitted that he feared invading me sexually, that he was constantly haunted by the fear of overwhelming me. The ugliness with which his mother had cursed him hindered any positive representation of his sex, leaving a gap that made him clumsy and awkward. From then on, when an emotion invaded him, he was gripped by the anxiety of being overwhelming. He thus forced himself to not become cumbersome, just as when he was young and he wanted to become invisible as a way of dealing with his mother's distaste for him. Many jealous people have had similar experiences. "It's because I'm ugly that she'll love another, better-looking man," one guy might say, wild with jealousy over a handsome rival. He may have an image of an ugly sexual body if his mother didn't invest in him in a loving manner. The father's gaze, the pride he experiences in belonging to his sex, and the femininity of his wife play essential roles in the love each of us has for our sexual self. Without these loving acknowledgments, the body remains a pile of ugly, uninhabited flesh. Apparently abandoned to a mother who did not look at him, David quelled his pain and his anger by reducing the field of his sensuality to a voyeuristic gaze. He had stopped investing his energy in his body since he had never been given the right to let it exist. His apathetic, absent body responded to erotic and voyeuristic arousal by saying "I am there for no one."

Jealous temperaments maintain a constant volleying between love and destructiveness, but David's violence had been completely silenced. This violence, which is essential for liberation from one's parents' unconscious issues, had instead turned back on itself. Because David was never jealous, he felt no anger or hatred.

Choosing a third path, David had sacrificed his body, had made a wasteland of it, conforming to the ugliness that his mother declared at his birth. Making himself ugly could be read as masochism. Having become a thing in his mother's eyes, he was in dire need of a helping hand in order to detach himself from her.

At the heart of his fantasy of making a woman happy he had lost pride by not being a man. The abstract entity of women, which was openly idealized, constituted a shield behind which he could hide. Since our first meeting, I had felt an almost hypnotic domination from him. Did this hypnotic shield have the ability to petrify the internal/mental life of the one who was exposed to it? David seemed to imitate the concerns of a perfect mother to the point of suffocation, as if to demonstrate how his mother had killed all the life in him.

"My mother constantly ran down men and my father used to listen without saying anything. I wanted to leave her but he beat me to it. He left my mother in my arms. He's the bastard!" David confessed, finally expressing all his anger by talking about his father, another man like him. He at last exhumed the fragments of his fallen masculine identity. This may explain why he had sobbed when he saw those dying men and women in Géricault's painting, a painful reminder of the abandonment into which he had fallen.

What role had his father played such that his son felt so insubstantially supported in his identity as a man?

A FATHER'S RESIGNATION

Confronted with his mother's refusal to recognize his young virility, David needed his father as a model and support in order to construct his sexual identity. Yet David's silence about his father left me confused.

When I told David I planned to go away on vacation, I noticed that he offered to collect my mail, as if, because I was a woman, he had to serve me too. I asked him, "Are you worried that your analyst is going away?" "Er . . . er . . ." he stammered, "I'm embarrassed about what I thought when you told me you were leaving. I wasn't happy. It wasn't anticipated. I didn't understand why you were heading off on this trip. I er . . . noticed your surname . . . well, I don't know . . . some impression I got . . . I thought . . . dirty . . . dirty . . . damned dirty Jew, there you go!" I burst into laughter on hearing these words, all the more so on seeing his embarrassment in proffering an insult rather than a vow of his attachment.

I pointed out that in order to express his anger, he resorted to insults that he himself disavowed. It was yet another way to put himself in the wrong.

His father was Jewish; his mother was not. She had kept this fact from David, and it was only at his father's funeral that he learned of his origins. "That bastard, that bastard!" David exclaimed. "He told me nothing about it, do you understand? And when my mother pissed me off, he told me to humble myself before her to ask her forgiveness!" Reluctantly, he reported to me a humiliating memory from his adolescence. "On your knees!" his father had one day instructed him. "Get down on your knees before your mother to beg her forgiveness!" David had just argued with her over a matter of little importance: he had refused to wear the ridiculously childish clothes she had bought for him. David received his father's words like a betrayal; he humbled himself on his knees.

To tell me about this humiliation proved to be a real test for David. Scolded by his father, he saw himself reduced to nothing, yet it was impossible for David to refuse him. Faced with this senseless situation, David had sought a solution to help keep himself going. In order to survive, he had had to swallow his rage. His cry for revenge was silent, a terrible mute shout.

I then pointed out to him that in the relationships he had begun with women, he had killed two birds with one stone. He had found a way to respond to both his parents at once. He took his revenge on his mother by reducing women to his mercy, and on his father by inverting the command he'd received (on your knees before your mother) into a new command that he voluntarily inflicted on himself (I will kneel down before all women's desires).

This situation, however, did not allow him to construct a solid and stable identity. His masculine image did not find a model with which to prop itself up. His father refused to provide such an image and thus confined his son to wandering. The latter could find no way out except by exhibiting a body sheltered from any feeling: he felt nothing, and especially no jealousy. From this empty, anonymous space where his masculine identity was barred and ruined, he could not be jealous.

ARTIFICIAL VIRILITY AND A TRUE FEMININE POSITION

If father and son had been close, David's father would have been able to create a common space with his son. He would have appeased the anxieties that were created from the maternal refusal of the young boy's sexuality. The father's failure to identify with his child, his inability to get close to him, had turned David's unsurprising aggressiveness toward his father into a silent hatred for himself.

A child's amorous dependency on his father (or on the man who takes his place) allows for exploration of a necessary position in the life of a man. It was what Freud called the boy's "inverted Oedipus." It permits the boy to acknowledge that an attitude said to be feminine does not necessarily lead to disaster. In other words, a boy's ability to face the unknown depends on paternal support, even if for the boy it means enjoying a father's love as well as using him as a model of how to become a man.

Only a terrain of understanding between a father and son can calm these primitive fears. It is not surprising therefore that so many men regret not sharing a bond of friendly complicity with their fathers, and this absence leaves them intensely nostalgic. David's father's attitude created a distance that was impregnated with fear, even a form of violence tinged with sadism. For David, unable to share anything with his father, nothing was strong enough to help him grasp that the unconscious nature of his mother's hatred did not concern him. Terrified, he had approached women in the same way that an animal-tamer sticks his head in a lion's jaw.

"Dirty Jew!" was addressed to the father who had kept his origins secret, and to his mother, the "dirty goy" to whom his father had abandoned him. This expression allowed David to explore fantasies that he had until then amputated. By stigmatizing his ugliness, did his mother not also address herself to the Jew in him? On top of the absence of masculine solidarity, did his father's estrangement also signify his exclusion from the family heritage? What sexual position could he have if he was totally cut off and severed from the roots of his same-sex parent? What way out was left for him, except to be jealous of his father's people?

This jealousy had fallen under the blow of real denial. If David now knew of his origins, this knowledge remained formal and empty. His father had not permitted him to associate with any part of it; on the contrary, he had excluded him. The analysis gave him the chance to flesh out this part of himself and this heritage that he had received, despite his father.

The fantasized narrative of our origins is unconsciously elaborated inside us. It is there that we place the strength of our identifications, even if they are conflicting. David's erotic game consisted of re-creating an encounter between a man and a woman (his father and his mother) while replaying the disappointment of being only the passive and powerless spectator. As a child he had assisted in his parents' life without ever having been invited in or authorized to participate. Faced with the impossibility of being their son, his lack of jealousy marked him as a human being incapable of desire or anger. His jealousy could not find expression because there was a need that was even greater: he needed to understand why he had come into the world. He had to fill in the gaps of what he knew of his origins so that he could inject erotic pleasure into his life. This could only happen if he could justify that his parents had at least a modicum of joy between them and thus that could explain in part why he had come into the world.

Having understood why his father had abandoned him and being reconnected with his Jewish heritage, David could finally identify with his father and no longer feel like the powerless victim of his mother's depressing denouncements. His father was no longer a stranger to him. But for David to change his position toward women, he first had to experience the pangs of jealousy in order to rescue himself from his apathy. Only then could the path of his desire be rediscovered.

A CASE OF BENEFICIAL JEALOUSY

A child can end up thinking that the otherness he represents in his parents' eyes is criminal. David described himself as a crab, an image borrowed from a drawing he had glimpsed in my office. As opposed to the drawing that showed a child proudly straddling a crab's shell to head out into the world, he saw himself as turned on his back, weakly wriggling his legs, waiting for the good will of a passerby who would put him back on his feet. I was the passerby who was going to approach him and draw him out of his apathetic body. I enabled him for the first time, in the space of the transference, to finally experience the true feeling of jealousy.

"I thought that you had a husband and how lucky he is!" he concluded one day. As I asked him to tell me more, he let his rage burst out: "I'm sure you two are as thick as thieves!" The insult had given space for his jealousy. His formula, "how lucky he is," let me see that he imagined himself as a rival, that he had authorized himself to enter into the amorous game instead of remaining the passive spectator. The expression "thick as thieves" evoked at once the two parents, the normal jealousy of the child excluded from their erotic game, but also his appetite to become a "thief" himself. Through his jealousy, David wanted to be recognized as like his parents. I pointed out to him that he was their child and thus had been like them all along.

A parent's hatred doesn't leave one indifferent, especially when it remains implied and not verbalized. Profound and often unnoticed disagreements, relationships founded on submissions that are never accepted, mourning that is never overcome or confronted all become the source of insurmountable enigmas. The child avows through loyalty to tolerate these enigmas, but he can come to lose his feeling of solidarity with his parents if he encounters a position that is untenable for him.

As we've seen, jealous individuals live outside of themselves, but are tortured; jealousy bears witness to a suffering that has no place to settle down. David's pain recalls the wounding loss of a part of himself that was stored, for lack of better options, in another loved one who always threatened to leave or betray him.

David had responded to his parents by reducing his body to abjection and trying to make any woman happy, no matter what. The strategies of cancelling out his suffering had at the same time cancelled out his jealousy. The pain of having no place of his own to exist as a sexual being was played out (and thus made unreal) in the sexual register where he contented himself with a simple voyeuristic gaze.

David was like the dying child in *The Raft of the Medusa*. He awaited something from me other than a medusa-like gaze, a gaze that he had tried to provoke by paralyzing me in our first meeting. But he had simply challenged me to bring him back to life.

CHAPTER 7

RIVALRY WITH ONE'S MOTHER: THE STORY OF PAULA

Paula was a young woman in her twenties who came to see me because she was experiencing such misery in her relationships. At her most jealous, Paula felt overcome by the need to rifle through her lover's pockets and drawers in search of a sign of his infidelity. Was she looking for proof that he was cheating on her? She believed this to be the case. Indeed, Paula's behavior exemplified the unremitting worries that upset the lives of jealous people of both sexes.

However, on listening more attentively to Paula, I realized that the aim of her behavior was, primarily, to gain access to the masculine domain: "I like to look at his ties too, to touch them. By spying on his world," she said, "I breathe him in. He who is man, who is masculine. When I don't know what something is, or I can't decipher the meaning of unreadable scribbles in his notebook, for example, I go mad with jealousy. I spend hours trying to work out what he's written, even going so far as to cross-examine him. During these moments I become very excited sexually."

PROBING THE MYSTERIES OF VIRILITY

What was the point of this behavior? Nothing seemed to appease Paula's desire to know what the other felt, thought, or expressed, and an unimaginable confusion tortured her. Exploring all of her lover's nooks and crannies, she wanted to touch a man, to have access to his mysteries. Overwhelmed by the other sex, she felt alive and excited in this search.

"Man's planet," as Paula called it, seemed all the more mystifying to her since her mother had kept her at a respectable distance from her own intimate relationships, as if her daughter should not approach this world under any condition. For this reason, men appeared to belong exclusively to her mother's territory—a private hunting ground, of sorts. "How did I not become a lesbian?" she often asked me. She marveled at the fact that she had not renounced her own attractiveness to men, or her own attraction to them, in order to leave the path clear for her mother. She was terrified of this dreadful rivalry that she suspected existed with her mother. Paula's father had left her and her mother to move to New Zealand when Paula was two years old, and since then she had not heard from him. According to her mother, he had rebuilt his life and had a son with another woman. "You see, sons stay with their fathers and daughters with their mothers!" her mother said one day, laughing. The young girl was deeply pained by this remark, and in her dreams she was convinced that her father would have taken her to the Antipodes if, by some chance, she had been a boy.

Because she excelled in sports and preferred running over drawing, she was always told that she was a tomboy. In addition, her desire to become a woman didn't hold much appeal. Without openly enjoying the benefits of her femininity, Paula never considered that perhaps her lover aroused a frantic search for the male part of herself simply because he was a man.

In the course of psychoanalysis, the patient is bound to encounter the ghosts that lie at the root of his or her suffering. By identifying them and driving them out, the patient becomes less attracted to them. Were there ghosts that guided Paula's tireless quest? Her mother, I found out, had been abused by her uncle and hated herself for having been subjected to this incest. Her shame, which transformed itself into self-hatred, thwarted her role in her daughter's developing femininity. The jealousy that pushed Paula to behave in such a seemingly absurd manner was in fact an attempt to penetrate not only her lover's sexual world, but also her own. This feverish search, however, only gave her access to a form of anxiety-filled excitement, which left her unsatisfied and bereaved. This, then, is the paradox of jealousy: it relentlessly poses questions without providing the possibility of a real solution.

In her adolescence, Paula had had a slight crush on her literature teacher, a woman who looked like her mother. Because of this, her mother had threatened to send her to boarding school. Convinced that her mother thought she was a lesbian, Paula had made the choice not to be one. "Men seem alien to me!" she often complained. But because she was happy with her male relationships, I found it difficult to give shape to her grievances. Sometimes she would address me, in turn furious or tormented: "You too, you're an alien! To seduce a man isn't a problem for you. You belong to that species from which I am completely estranged: Women!"

She wasn't "like the rest of them," she complained, because she didn't know how to seduce a man, "snatch him up, effortlessly, like women know how to do. They arrive, do a little trick, snap their fingers, and snatch him up . . . !" She also complained of not having had the opportunity to dazzle her father. "In two years of life shared with my father, I never really got to know him. He didn't take me diving like my friend Y.'s dad did, he didn't explain anything to me about men, I never saw him do what men do, play soccer . . . all that!" Paula felt excluded from a man's world.

She was not wrong. Her father had disappeared very early in her life. Paula, however, despite her denying it, seemed wholly feminine to me. She expressed a real desperation through her fantasies about my erotic life. Yet it was not so much that the masculine universe was unknown to her, rather that what she was really lacking was an understanding of the feminine universe. Although she handled the analysis with intelligence and grace, I noticed how carefully she treated me. She seemed to try to take up as little space as possible, to not bother me under any pretext, to construct an invisible wall between us. I pointed this out to her on one occasion, that she seemed to handle me as one would a fragile or cumbersome object. In an unconscious way, was it my femininity that seemed unapproachable and drove her to steer clear of it? I lost myself in conjectures, often irritated by the feeling that our work suffered on account of her lack of spontaneity.

THE ENIGMA OF STOLEN FEMININITY

When Paula and I resumed our work together after a lengthy vacation, she asked to speak to me face to face, rather than from her usual position of lying on the couch. I accepted, intrigued. During the holidays she had had two dreams in which several people had wanted to rob me of personal objects. In the one she remembered more vividly, I confronted the robbers, which relieved her a great deal. She then informed me that the interruption of our analytical work had given her the chance to meet an older man, with whom she had fallen very much in love. But the rummaging had begun again, without any apparent motive, and she no longer understood her persistence in needlessly delving into her lover's privacy.

In one part of Paula's dream, the thieves were robbing me; in the other, I defended myself against them. Did she fear that I might accuse her of theft if she had a happy sexual life, and at the same time, did she dread not being able to protect her new relationship (from me)? As Paula was uncertain whether she was able to distinguish between reality and fiction, I wondered whether meeting each other face to face was necessary for her to verify that her fears were unfounded. I then asked her if she had wished to see me face to face to assure herself, with her own eyes, that nothing had been stolen, from her or from me, because she now loved a man.

When she heard me evoke the possible coexistence of our two erotic lives, a smile lit up her face. It reminded her of an incident that took place when she was sixteen, out on a walk with her mother in Spain. A man had walked by them and, just as he passed, shouted, "*Guapa* (beautiful)!" Her mother had taken the compliment for herself, but Paula had felt the man's hand on her hip and had understood that the homage was directed toward her.

Why didn't she say anything? She thought her mother would take offense. In other circumstances, her mother kept her daughter away from her relationships with men and then accused her of clinging to her, blaming her for the fact that she was without a man. Paula had to renounce nearly all sexual feelings for fear of stealing from her mother. But if her erotic life wasn't allowed to be established, she found herself, in turn, robbed of the means of being a woman. She thus rifled through her lover's closets to find the thing that had been stolen from her. Many jealous men and women complain of having been displaced and stripped by a rival. Men willingly convince themselves that such a rival has a phallic power that assures him the pleasure of every woman. Women, however, are more inclined to believe that the other sex has a weakness for all femininity but their own. In the jealous individual's mind the other has an impenetrable secret. The jealous person then suffers from the impossibility of accessing it.

A MOTHER'S MAD RIVALRY

If one takes the jealous individual's complaints seriously, the theft he or she feels is certainly an imaginary one, but it bears witness to a very real injury. His or her identity is bruised, a sign that it has been insufficiently loved and acknowledged. Paula probed her lover's secrets in the vain hope of finding out the truth about the masculine. Her jealousy was then sparked by the mystery of a few incomprehensible words that she had interpreted to be particularly hostile. The delirious excitement of her search suggests that Paula gave herself the right to steal because her mother had never allowed her access.

The circumstances of Paula's jealousy give an indication that her interest in masculinity was paired with something forbidden: her own sexuality. Rivalry with her mother had never been resolved; this is, surely, the reason she treated me so carefully. Paula showed that she was incapable of contemplating a common ground with the feminine Eros. The jealous person's desire shines a light on the conditions of every person's desire: to have been loved by her mother, not only as a little girl, but also as a woman in the making. Women who have been deprived of this gift are more prone to jealousy. From their despised rival, they await the keys to the erotic dimension of their sex, an expectation that is of course impossible to satisfy, but that reveals what has been missing in these women's sexual awakening. By compulsively rummaging through her lover's drawers, Paula searched to encounter her rival, someone to confront, certainly, but above all someone to meet and get to know.

The rivalry between a mother and daughter merits some attention. On first glance, it was an excess of rivalry between Paula and her mother that had prohibited her from competing with her mother. Rivalry indicates that a veritable rival is recognized.

Such a rivalry is beneficial because it offers a framework in which the girl can measure herself against her mother/rival and work out identification and differentiation.

On the other hand, by designating the young girl or boy as the mother's or father's rival, the tension (which is born from a mother's or father's own anxiety about her or his sexual identity) inhibits and freezes the child with terror; she or he can no longer play at competing with Mommy or Daddy. The game of identification is hindered by the terror of winning a battle in which he or she never intended to engage.

What existed between Paula and her mother was a great step away from the normal rivalry between a woman and her daughter. For the mother, the challenge was real. A veritable adversary in this woman's eyes, Paula could no longer distinguish where reality lay. If the distinctions between dream and reality, between the internal and external worlds, seemed so difficult for her to make, it was because the symbolic reference points that gave them structure had been gravely damaged. Mixing the language of the child and of the adult, the positions of mother and daughter, that of men and women, Paula's mother perpetrated a harmful state of confusion.

When Paula allowed herself to protest how her mother was dismissive of her, the latter rejected her, calling her protests ingratitude or unfounded fictions. In this way, Paula remained trapped in her relationship with her mother, without a third person to help her get a reality check. Her space of feminine thought and existence found itself invaded and uncertain.

WOUNDED FEMININITY, MATERNITY HELD IN CONTEMPT

No doubt shattered and terrified by the violent incest she herself had undergone, Paula's mother was incapable of transmitting to her daughter the notion that men can bring pleasure and relief to a woman's sexual cravings; any hope of positive bodily pleasure was quashed. Did this woman unconsciously envy her daughter for having had what she herself had missed out on since she was herself sexually abused as a child? Not having received the necessary protection to negotiate the vicissitudes of her own sexuality, how could she in turn take care of her daughter's femininity? Whatever the case, she probably submitted her daughter to a sexual rivalry at far too young an age.

In Paula's case, she did not merely transfer her mother's jealousy onto her lovers. Her jealousy was a response to the destructive effects of her mother's projections and hindered the construction of a feminine identity. The young girl had lived her oedipal rivalry to such an extent that, in her eyes, her mother seemed unpredictable and impenetrable. Later she would perceive every woman touched by a man's desire in this same way: the woman would metamorphose into an alien, all-powerful and inaccessible. Jealousy brought Paula down to ground level, abandoning her without words on an "unknown planet" that resembled the feminine land to which she was forbidden entry. By compulsively rummaging through her lover's drawers, dazzled and attracted by the masculine, Paula managed to appropriate the male mysteries about which her mother had forbidden her to ask.

For a mother, a female child can represent that part of her femininity that she delights in. Through her caresses, a mother touches the child's body and thus eroticizes it. She is the first to make the child aware of her body's boundaries. But this confrontation between mother and daughter had not been played out for Paula on the register of pleasure, but on the one of prejudice and hurt.

Paula's mother was unable to invest an eroticized maternal presence in her daughter without destroying herself, because she had not been protected from familial incest by her own mother.

This caused her to have a profound resentment toward the motherly function. She expressed her contempt by endlessly mocking her daughter's full hips, saying they resembled those of the peasants of the Mediterranean countryside of her childhood.

"It's not so much you that she dislikes, but more likely, the maternal role that she hates," I said to Paula one day in response to her hopelessness. Paula then understood that her mother's remark about her large hips was aimed beyond her, at an abhorred maternal figure represented by those wide-hipped statuettes of the ancient fertility goddesses. This interpretation helped her see the difference between her mother's envy of her and her mother's distaste for the maternal role. It also helped Paula feel free to enjoy her own feminine charms.

REUNITING WITH PATERNAL LANDMARKS

When a girl is not touched in a happy and loving way by her mother's gaze and hands, her femininity remains in an inaccessible elsewhere. Jealousy uses its destructive force to negate any representation of her body, leaving a void in its place. Paula's mother lacked, at the very least, some sense of solidarity, and this left her daughter hanging in suspense. The mother seemed to own everything and Paula nothing.

Paula often reproached me for belonging to a feminine "species" of which she was not a part. Tirelessly rifling through her lover's pockets, she was vainly hunting for this possession, as precious as it was inaccessible. At the same time, she was maniacally searching for the paternal points of reference that were buried in the depths of her mother's accusations about the father who had abandoned her.

As a witness to the mute drama of her childhood, I made Paula realize that questions of love and eroticism could be shared with other women without their robbing her. From then on, I was able to show her that the masculine universe was within her reach, and she had no more need to fruitlessly rummage in any drawers.

Although the small girl had not had a lot of time to be with her father, she did have two years, she said to me laughing. "Two years, it's quite a long time! Longer than it should take to charm a man, don't you think?" Paula's femininity had been triggered into motion again, and if she set out to prove to herself that she could seduce a man in no time at all, or in less time than it took to say it, I was certainly not going to blame her for it.

It is a difficult experience for a girl to be like her mother while at the same time her rival. Yet both these states, although incompatible, are necessary. Mother and daughter, the one and the other, the one for the other, have to invent a space of solidarity where each one's originality rests on the emphasis of what is common between them. This is a very difficult task if the feminine is devalued by dominant cultural representations, and all the more so if one or the other of the pair has undergone degrading cases of violence that engender a profound sense of shame.

The formation of sexual identity is an essential piece in understanding jealousy: indeed, a mother may feel deep ambivalence toward her daughter because she represents for the mother a younger self who has a life separate from her. Subjected to the maternal wavering between love and hate of the daughter's sexual evolution, a girl will feel these vacillations like a weighty pile of mysteries that bear down on her feminine evolution.

MOTHERS' DIFFERENT FORMS OF JEALOUSY

Maternal love, far from being angelic, is an impassioned love unconsciously laced with violence. It is a love of hopes and regrets, but also a love that soothes and caresses. It is in this way that a mother is present for her children and summons them to live. Paradoxically, a mother normally loves her son or daughter a bit like a lion, and suffers from envy of the adult life that he or she will have without her. She might think: "another woman will be in my son's arms" or "another man will embrace my daughter." From then on, the child is no longer the mother's child, but a young man or a young woman. This differentiation is at work from the time of birth onward. From that point, the mother endures a form of suffering that needs to be overcome. It is a difficult stage not only for the child who, recognized as a sexed being, finds herself alone, but also for her mother, who anticipates the moment when her child will find love elsewhere.

Thus there is a parallel between maternal jealousy and what has been said of a child's jealousy. A mother is always left somewhat destitute at the birth of her child, severed from the fantasy of being one with her. To contain the pain of such a loss, transforming jealousy into the joy of discovering the future, is the work of love that every mother offers each time she gives birth. When a mother can overcome the natural jealousy she feels toward her child, she will be greatly rewarded by this process. It is almost impossible for a mother not to experience at some point or another some difficulties in her impassioned investment in her child. However, when these difficulties are further hindered by an earlier trauma, motherhood can become a real burden. This certainly explains Paula's mother's extreme jealousy and her inability to go through the movement of separation through which a child is loved not as same but as other.

An unhealthy jealousy is the sign of an incestuous enjoyment that binds the child hand and foot, and expresses an implacable tyranny. For the development of a girl's sexuality, her mother's frenzied jealousy can be disastrous. For a boy too, although differently. A mother may perceive a son as incarnating an ideal of masculinity. Because she resents him for what she is not, her son will in turn have an inclination toward depression and sadistic tendencies. A boy cannot love himself as a little man if his mother is conflicted with her own sex. The way in which a mother loves, or doesn't, her own feminine and erotic self is fundamental for the erotic future of both boys and girls. In one way or another, the self-hatred that haunts a mother will be projected more or less openly onto her child, of whatever sex, and will seem to be directed against his or her sexual evolution. The bodily emotions, closely shared with the mother at the beginning of life, will thus be frozen. Such a child won't be able to recognize himself in the worth of his own sex, or learn that the other sex is within his reach.

In light of the idealization of the maternal function, pervasive in all cultures, it is important to emphasize the erotic connection between mother and child. Yet, jealousy underlies it. A mother who does not experience her own femininity as pleasurable will have trouble assuming her role as a mother who can love in her children their own erotic impulses. When she does, she will also feel jealous of the little boy's future loves, or the little girl's beauty different from her own. A mother's normal amorous jealousy is thus the flip side of the acceptance of her own gender and sexuality—of the acceptance of the sexed in oneself.

Maternal jealousy is always "sexed"

Normal maternal jealousy is related to sex because a boy or a girl is loved in his future sexuality, distinct from that of his mother, but it also implies that boys and girls are loved by their mother in both their masculine and feminine sides.

The maternal function is to provide the space of mediation between the child and the ideals or obstacles that his body encounters. For example, a mother can hand down to her daughter the unconscious hatred that she feels toward herself as a woman. Despite the fact that the masculine sex is favored in most societies, women have used, time and again, strategies to transmit to their children the erotic joys of femininity and their pride in its power. A mother's bisexual love toward her child imposes the value of the feminine erotic. Thanks to mothers, the denial of the feminine isn't necessarily passed down to their children.

A mother, therefore, needs a healthy dose of jealousy in order to recognize the potential of her child's sexual desire. The normally jealous mother senses her child's seduction and loves it more than she resists it. In this way, she embodies a jealousy that is erotic. This sufficiently good jealousy is possible only if the previous generations haven't transmitted a hatred of sexual pleasure. But if the other sex remains, to a greater or lesser degree, an ominous unknown and sexuality is seen as something to be tamed, hatred and fear can easily take hold.

The pain of a mother's normal jealousy, which begins each time she gives birth, and the work it imposes are thus made of love. The mother loves her child not only as a mother who feels at one with her child, but also as a woman who feels separate from her boy or girl. In the process she may feel jealous of her daughter's beauty or of her son's masculine power. To be torn between her calling as mother and her wish to keep in touch with her womanhood is the plight that any mother confronts at one time or another. This difficult work of both connecting and separating from her child is crucial insofar as children must experience their mothers not only as caregivers but also as women who derive other pleasures in life than the sight of their progeny. A mother's heroic struggle to keep in check all the facets of her desire can only help foster her children's capacity to have fulfilling sexual and loving relationships in the future.

CHAPTER 8

LILY: BISEXUAL AND JEALOUS

"When she looks at someone else, she is insulting me, so I have the right to do whatever I want," said Lily, who dreamed of wiping out her rivals. The moment her female lover caught the eye of another woman, Lily exploded into a fit of jealousy, confessing that she couldn't stop herself. "When I'm in love, I'm a different person, a madwoman," she confessed. Lily, a woman in her forties, had come to see me because of her violent outbursts. Her impulsiveness had calmed down a bit now that she was with a new companion, but the relationship that her lover had with her old girlfriend was exasperating her. "She drives me wild, I'm beside myself," she told me. "She talks to her every day, when she's not meeting up with her on the sly, using my jealousy as an excuse, so that we don't bump into each other. Sometimes I manage to forget, but at other moments, I don't know why, jealousy stirs inside me and I harass her, almost to prove that it's her behavior that is the cause of all of this." Feeling as if nothing could stop her in these moments, Lily thought that she could kill somebody and she often made ardent, indiscriminate threats of death if she were to discover her lover with another.

Her attitude toward her present lover was no different from the one she had had toward her former boyfriends. "I've always been jealous," she added, "that's just the way I am." Homosexuality, latent or not, unconscious or acted upon, does nothing to change jealousy. Furthermore, male or female homosexuals are no less jealous than those who proclaim to love the opposite gender, but no more so either.

Lily wasn't only distressed by her jealousy, she was also embarrassed by a certain difficulty with her sexuality. When, through perseverance, she managed to separate her boyfriends from other girlfriends so that they dedicated themselves entirely to her, her interest in them disappeared. Even now, as soon as she had won over her girlfriends, her desire for them promptly dried up. The realization of her desire became an impossible feat: it was an absolute torture for as long as she felt excluded from the magic cradle of those she loved. Yet she lost her passion as soon as she got her way.

This is a classic dilemma. Many men and women in love admit that the chase and acquisition impassions them far more than the routine of love. For many, passion and routine are in opposition, and the feeling of jealousy at least has the value of revealing their dormant desire to them. These people, so busy inventing hypothetical cases of betrayal in an attempt to sustain their waning fervor, don't acknowledge or question the tendency toward boredom at the heart of their relationships. Their desire is driven by the conquest of a man or a woman under the sole (but compelling) condition that their lover has to be dragged away from a third person. The third party vanquished, the desire vanishes.

DESIRE'S BEST FRIEND

Psychoanalysts ordinarily focus more on the triangular relationships that give rise to jealousy than on the struggle undertaken by the jealous individual against a rival. Is this reminiscent of the child's exclusion from the sexual life of the parents, another inaccessible pair? Not quite. What Lily revealed is that jealousy was not a mere rivalry with a person capable of stealing the object of love (the father or the mother depending on the case) or a wish to vanquish her competitor. For her, desire dwindled when there was no longer a rival on the horizon. It was the day-to-day intimacy that Lily found dreadful and seemed to be the cause of the disappearance of her desire. "It's down there that I have issues. When I live side by side with a man or woman, the moment I am naked, I feel unhappy, ugly, and empty," she said, hesitating, before admitting that she liked "to give pleasure, not to receive it." For as long as the rival remained an obstacle, amorous intimacy with a man or woman didn't seem at all dangerous. She concentrated on the competition, only interested in the challenge of winning over her prey. On the other hand, once she had gotten rid of her adversaries, the intimacy of bodies became menacing for her, as she found herself feeling alone before her lovers. Without her hated and envied rivals, she felt exposed and defenseless, *naked*, *ugly*, and *empty*. Contrary to what one might expect, it was the presence of a rival that protected her from the void of her sexual body, this awkwardness *down there*.

This feeling of being sexually ugly that occurs frequently in the discourse of homo- or heterosexual jealous individuals, bears witness to a narcissistic wound. Their jealousy is therefore less a result of the repression of a homosexual desire than the hope to have their sexuality acknowledged as man or woman. This attempt to restore some form of narcissism with the help of an imaginary prop (the rival figure) does not, however, take into account the extinguishing of desire that occurs when all reasons for jealousy have disappeared. In Lily's case, the *real* presence of her rival seemed to be a necessary condition so that the erotic games of desire might appeal to her. Without a rival underfoot, Lily couldn't create erotic fantasies for herself, where she could play at being active or passive. The excitement brought on by jealousy likewise revealed the void that her jealousy masked and filled.

Paradoxically, Lily's jealousy, which in outward appearance seemed to be linked to the presence of an intruder at the center of her relationships, was less a competitive jealousy than a jealousy that hoped to preserve the existence of an erotic desire and an erotic body.

THE LOVERS' BEDROOM

The child becomes jealously aware of her parents' sexual prowess and feels terribly depressed, observing that she does not yet possess these powers, but her dreams are filled with what she imagines happens in this dark room. Adults' sexual lives, when not exhibited or acted out in front of the child, become for her a boundless source of fantasies. When assured that the parents are erotically content, the child's momentary jealousy is likely to disappear, along with her anger at feeling excluded.

A mother's or father's eroticism humanizes the roles they play, and they then seem to be just regular people, happy or unhappy, and in any case less awe-inspiring. The child figures out for herself that these sexual privileges will be hers in a foreseeable future. Besides, the fact that the child is excluded from the adults' sexual lives is not the major cause of her jealousy. She does not want to be a part of a sexual life that she cannot even fathom. Rather, it is the absence of eroticism between her parents that wounds her. She feels exiled, having nothing to feed her dream of delights for when she grows up. Instead she excites herself with howls of jealousy while her erotic body remains frozen.

Jealousy's flames permit her to draw the body out of this ice cage. This impassioned trait that ties jealous men and women to their rivals expresses an anxiety about the annihilation of the self.

CARESSING INSECTS

A recurring nightmare that Lily often had at the most intense points of her anguish helped me understand more about this annihilation. In this dream, some sort of insect approached her. Without being able to see it, she felt the gentle beating of its wings rubbing along the length of her neck. She then awakened, seized by an unspeakable terror. When I interpreted "its wings rubbing along the length of her neck," Lily understood that the terror that this nightmare awakened came from those "caresses that weren't seen." Who did she not see when she was a child? This question brought forth the memory of her mother's lovers, who were always hidden, carefully and with a particular pleasure. Her mother led an apparently animated extramarital life. Without putting it into words, she demanded that her daughter not tell her father. Lily was thus implicated in the secret. Like every child, she had been attentive to the signs of her mother's femininity, and had searched to grasp the mystery of the bond between her parents. As a girl, Lily would have liked to have shared with her mother not her sexual life, but the joy of feminine and masculine pleasures. The act of complicity that her mother forced upon her, however, made the hope of such sharing impossible because this mother would have scoffed at her loyalty to her father.

A dream becomes a nightmare when it gives rise to extreme anguish. One wakes from a nightmare because the story becomes unbearable. The proliferation of invisible and menacing insects in Lily's dream was sparked by a prohibition—the wish to have access to something that had to remain hidden. The great delight that Lily's mother took in concealing her erotic life represented a devastating mystery to her daughter. And it was the invisibility of her mother's sexuality that was nightmarish.

As in the tale of Cinderella, Lily's mother, still young and beautiful, flaunted her allure in front of her daughter. Adorned like a queen, she enjoyed making her daughter a "lady's maid" who then remained alone and forgotten at home when her father was traveling. Able to see her mother's preparations, she was unable to know anything about them. Reduced to a gaze, she could only imagine in silence the ballet of lovers who never came into view. In her eyes, they seemed all the more grandiose and threatening as they had the power to draw her mother away from her. This traumatic fear of abandonment that haunts all childhoods was awakened and projected onto these men.

Lily's mother said she had a right to have a private life and didn't want to sacrifice her life as a woman. But what was damaging for Lily was that through her hidden life, this woman organized a staunch rivalry between her lovers and Lily. And because it was never spoken of, this rivalry plunged her daughter into the absurd and caused her hatred. Not that this mother should have shown her lovers to her daughter, but the unspoken complicity that the mother demanded of her daughter ruined any real exchange that they could have had. Such refusal to talk, or explain what she was asking from Lily, placed Lily in an impossible situation: to know and not to know, to see and not to see. The situation also took on the significance of a major and conflicting prohibition for Lily: to be or not to be a woman. So that Lily could continue to desire, so that a favorable framework might exist for the elaboration of her fantasies and dreams, a real woman, a rival, or a competitor became indispensable to her.

THE CONQUEST OF DESIRE

In order to stop the compulsive need for a rival, the jealous person must once again conquer her desire. Lily told me one day that she felt like a cat, "a wildcat." The atmosphere in the session was, as it often was, electric, but this time there was an aspect of fear and expectation merged with the tension. She remained silent. I was sensitive to the importance of this moment, because, if the signifier "cat" evoked the feminine sexual organs (pussy), it was a challenge for me to try and reactivate her desire as a woman. Up to this point, Lily's desire couldn't be aroused except through jealousy; she was irremediably cut off from it.

By inviting Lily to let the wildcat speak, I asked her what it was doing, what it wanted. "What's happening to it?" I said to her. "It is running, it is clawing the walls of your office," she said to me. "It's a hunted animal, in desperate straits. But it can turn around on that person who is chasing it and suddenly growl." She then added, "You're pursuing it. It can't bear any more of your questions!" I went silent. Finally Lily spoke again: "Are you still there? It was suddenly very cold and I thought you had gone." I was there, with her, in the space where the cat was running around on a rampage. She was both afraid that I chased after her and that I had abandoned her to the cold of absence. The erotic space began to exist once we found the right distance between the fear (and desire) of being seduced–pursued by the analyst-woman-mother-cat and the fear (and desire) of being abandoned to her mother's cold and untouchable sexuality.

The wild animal designated her sexuality; at last, she could let it run free. It was also allowed to fight back by growling at the person who was chasing her. Her question—"Are you there? It's suddenly cold"—evoked the absence of a warm maternal bond. She seemed to me to have lacked a mother who would have caressed her and looked upon her in a happy and loving manner. Her mother's femininity remained in an inaccessible elsewhere. Lily's confessed anxiety, that of being a solitary and abandoned pussycat, gave a glimpse of the layers of ice that had frozen and petrified her feminine childhood language.

Beyond her mother's iciness, across the common space of transference, the image of the cat not only allowed Lily to rekindle her desire to live, but also her sexual desire.

JEALOUS STIMULATION AS A BATTLE AGAINST DEPRESSION

A number of jealous men and women complain that their sexual or erotic lives elude them, that sexuality seems alien and cut off from the world of language. Jealousy, through substitution, provides many of them with a form of sexual stimulation to which they resort in order to compensate for this part of themselves that they cannot otherwise access. Fantasies are thus short-circuited, replaced by a permanent state of tension that almost physically attaches the jealous person to the one who incites the jealousy. Abandoning jealousy is difficult because it has a stimulating effect that enables the sufferer to battle depression. Many jealous types confess that calm relationships bore them; others manage to generate the same frame of mind in their companions, so that jealousy serves as the cement.

However exalting it may be, jealousy provokes a worrying sexual arousal that recalls what the young child once felt. At the same time, it keeps the jealous person on tenterhooks, awaiting appeasement, driving him to refuse, with a strength born of desperation, all that will bring him back to the calm flats of the depressive state. By dint of being a spectator to her mother, Lily knew these episodes of low spirits well.

Paradoxically, the absence of common sexual space between the child and her mother or father has the same wounding effect on childhood language as an abusive intrusion. The right distance is therefore required for a child to be able to elaborate in her mind some ideas about the mystery of sexuality.

It is the untamed characteristic of sexuality that often gives one a way out. Wild animal images, at once appealing and scary, allow the child of either sex to draw from them active sexual representations. Thanks to the freedom that these images evoke, the child can liberate herself from empty or mortifying evocations of eroticism. The emerging of the wildcat represented Lily's revolt against the obligation to reduce her desiring body to nothing.

Because only an interior experience of desire permits the individual to renounce her jealousy, one can understand why the analysis of certain jealous men or women falters. For them, the mystery of sexuality is seen only from the outside. Therefore they persist in waiting for their lovers, or even their analyst, to grant them the right to be a sexual woman or man. The analyst can offer a space in which sexual speech ceases to be excluded and from which desire can be reborn.

THE ANALYST'S LIGHTS

Through a dream, Lily resurrected a homosexual space that we were sharing. In the dream, my office resembled a shop of electrical supplies; faced with her surprise, I assured her that these instruments "were really very useful in life." Laughing, still in the dream, she then fondly corrected my words by remarking that "[my] lights were clearly a lot more than just useful!" She finished by tenderly putting her arms around me, stunned to feel my body, feline and supple, against her own.

Was the laughter, in the dream, not a sign of shared pleasure? The electrical accessories perhaps represented the electric sessions that I had been through with her. The establishing of a space of exchange between us inspired her hope to acquire other lights. Through this, Lily bore witness to her intense yearning to use her erotic feminine body wildly and freely, like a feline. The evoking of the feline and supple side of my body demonstrated an appropriation of her predatory desire. This dream can be read on two levels. On the one hand, it demonstrated the conquering of a happy relationship with a woman. On the other, the laugh affirmed that feline sexuality is joyously shared, so that her homosexual desire could be satisfied. It is difficult to transmit all the emotions that pass through one analytic session, but, whatever they were, Lily's body had ceased to be ugly or empty.

The jealous person uses jealousy as a stimulant, because she does not have access to the reveries or fantasies that would enable her to move freely between masculine and feminine identities. She has stopped short in her bisexuality, and jealousy keeps her in suspense. Jealous men and women, homosexual or heterosexual, share similar issues. Their sexual choices, whatever they may be, effectively obey the same rules: they seek to console and repair themselves, sometimes to wound themselves, and often believe they are overcoming their own limits. They make us realize that all sexuality can be utilized, due to its manic or compulsive dimension, to repair ills of a completely other nature. Therefore, the logic that leads to a feminine or masculine identity is not the same as the one that makes a person homosexual or heterosexual. There is an erotic bond between mother and daughter that is transmitted through love. Through her mother, the daughter learns what it means to be desired sexually.

If a girl first sees herself though her mother's eyes and loves herself in the way that her mother (but also her father) loves her—in and for her femininity—it is the mother's feminine erotic that is expressed in this homosexuality. This common sexual body had not been constructed between Lily and her mother.

As jealousy no longer served its purpose of stimulating her femininity, Lily could stop living her life according to it. Quite spectacularly, she agreed to meet her lover's former companion and found her delightful. All need to control the gaze of the one she loved had disappeared. The construction of a space in the analysis had been essential, as much to put an end to her jealousy as to unleash her erotic pleasure. Whether Lily finds these pleasures with a man or a woman isn't the question. What matters is that Eros has finally ceased to be full of sorrow.

CHAPTER 9

ENVY AND JEALOUSY IN THE LIFE OF JULIA

Julia was a beautiful twenty-something aspiring actress who had been coming to me for more than a year. During most of our sessions, she was courteous and determined, not leaving much room for anything unexpected.

"I'll think about it when I'm on my own," she used to say to me when I came up with a new suggestion. At other times she questioned me warily: "I sometimes think that you keep your thoughts to yourself instead of telling me." These words made me feel ill at ease. It is not my habit to be withholding, and my patients usually expect that I say what is on my mind. To listen deeply, without reserve, allows patients' unconscious memories to come to the surface. This type of listening creates an atmosphere of closeness that is different from the kind we encounter in ordinary life. If I wasn't saying everything to Julia, it was because I was discovering the terrain of her conflicts at the same time as she was revealing them. Also, she hastened to forget what I did say, only to later rediscover our few steps forward on her own, often retranslating my words into psychological jargon she had heard on some TV talk show.

Fortunately, I was able to lean on several tangible elements of our shared analytic journey so as not to feel swept off track by her reproaches. Her professional life clearly had improved since she started working with me, and she no longer let herself be exploited by friends and lovers as was her habit. Without noticing her own inconsistencies, Julia would accuse me of wasting her time because I kept all of my interpretations to myself, but she would just as likely thank me for the precious help the analysis had brought her. Then, when she might become aware of what she was saying, she would seek refuge in another line: "You're doing everything and I'm doing nothing. I'm an assistant. I depend completely on you. I don't understand anything about my life."

On one day, though, Julia began our session, not with her usual lively tone, but with an iciness. Submerged in anger, she almost choked with fury as she began to speak. "I didn't get any sleep last night," she exclaimed, exasperated, before bursting into curses against me. No one understood her, she fumed. "I'm doing everything in this analysis and I am falling into ruin!" she said, "and, on top of that, I have nothing. You're giving me nothing!"

Then, in a sudden outburst of rage that nothing could stop (nor would I try to), she began to scream that my office was so big. She literally bellowed, snorting with rage, "Who do you think you are?"

Trying to clear an opening, I risked asking her what my office evoked in her. My office is of a relatively average size; it's certainly not big. Julia barely responded to my questions, and I realized that any reference to reality upset her. She preferred to shout, insisting that she had touched on a taboo, that she shouldn't confront her analyst with this sort of truth.

While still listening, I tried to continue thinking despite her cries. Why does she suddenly find my office so big? Up to that point, Julia had never complained about anything. Could I have

misunderstood? Could she have concealed some financial difficulties? I was confused. Placing the blame on me, she exhibited wild envy that made me lose my train of thought. I resolved
to accept this puzzle on her terms without trying to solve the
mystery too quickly.

THE DESTROYED INTERNAL SPACE

The word *big* resounded that day in a deafening manner. I felt
invaded with noise, with her screamed responses. The outburst
of rage made the walls tremble, and I dreaded that this anger
might turn on her, as I felt she might shatter. Her envy of my
big office was laced with a deathly violence: nothing else existed.
She started to make a long detailed list of things I possessed: I
had everything, and she had nothing.

An idea then came to me, shedding a different light on her
envious rage. She had accosted me, attacking my things, my
walls, and thus also my interior and my body. Envy seemed to
highlight a forbidden and impossible contact between two beings.
Was this about two women or perhaps a mother and her daughter? It seemed clear that her aggression rested on something that
was common to both of us, but, at the same time, wasn't.

Julia made the real limits of my office bigger; she didn't just
content herself with attacking them, she *displaced* them. Her
fury, however, seemed like fantasy. She identified something that
made her mad, and I was only just beginning to understand.

In getting drawn into and overwhelmed by the dimensions
of *my* office, Julia tried to make it understood how her inner
world had been shattered. The fact that my office was suddenly
too big for her exposed the terrible force that destroys the symbolic framework in which one lives. Her rage wasn't just

destructive; it revealed a situation that was unbearable for her. Julia felt as if I was attacking her identity, making her feel small and unimportant. She could not find the words to express her feeling of inferiority; her only recourse was to attack my office. We cannot function in the world unless we have some stable sense of the space we occupy. Such space shapes the vision we have of ourselves. If this self-representation is shattered, we are left with despair and rage because there is an inexpressible gap between the way we used to feel when we were getting the recognition we sought and the sense of deprivation that follows.

By calling attention to the space of my office, Julia showed me (instead of telling me) that her foundations were under attack. She was lost because of it. Her rage began to seem legitimate and she screamed of a distress that did not yet have a name. My big office was Julia, it was she being attacked, deprived of the only nourishment that a person can feed on: recognition, presence, status. My big office represented her symbolic place as the eldest (the biggest) sister damaged by an assault whose origins I didn't yet know.

THE TURNING POINT OF THE ANALYSIS

I made Julia take note of the fact that she accused me of ruining her by feeding off her, which was the same reproach she made to her mother, who had taken everything from her, according to her claims. I reminded her of her need to think about this interpretation on her own. Was there some danger in thinking in my presence? Was I going to encroach on her prerogatives as the biggest, as an adult? I asked her again, "Do you think that I have no respect for *your* capacities to be big or that I belittle them?

Do you feel that the only way to affirm yourself, to wipe the slate clean of everything we exchange, is through your rage?" "I'm not allowed to talk about that!" she shouted in a terrified voice. "It's taboo, forbidden!"

"I'm not allowed to speak of the failings or the violence of your mother toward you? Not allowed to speak of you and her muddled together in your rage, just as I am tied to your anger?" I said to her.

Julia then calmed down. "I don't know what's wrong with me. I have some horrible things in my head, some things that are not right. I see my mother laughing when I realized she was pregnant. Her pregnancy was already very advanced, and she laughed and laughed. She laughed at my surprise. She had never said anything to me. Before, she counted on me for everything. She was scared of my father. I was her partner, her daughter, and her mother. I was *her* big one—she called me '*my* big girl.' But after my mother revealed her pregnancy to me, I was left out of the picture. My younger sister never looked at me as a big sister. I think it must have started at that moment. Yes! It's coming back to me: my mother started to call my younger sister 'my big girl' after her birth."

Julia's envy toward my office did not set its sights upon the good that I brought her through analysis; rather she clamored to be recognized by me. Although envy appeared to drive Julia to be destructive, ultimately, by exposing herself to me, she was awaiting a word of legitimization to restore her symbolic place as her mother's big girl.

As long as the people around Julia did not provide her with this essential recognition, she was condemned to relive her traumatic wound. My big office that she envied showed her desire to have an interior space where she would feel in the open and from where she could connect with others. She desperately searched to make this muted, misunderstood distress heard.

ENVY: AN EMERGENCY RESPONSE TO THE ANNOUNCEMENT OF A DISASTER?

Julia emphasized just how much she had suffered from her mother's withdrawal. More profoundly, she gave me a clue to the cause of the severe collapse of her identity. "I was left out, in a sort of vacant space," she had said, without suspecting the gravity of the state in which this had plunged her. She could not make sense of her mother's absurd laughter that had shattered her belief in her mother's love toward her. She had lost sight of her landmarks. Her existence had suddenly appeared meaningless. The word *big* held a lot of meaning for her.

When she was little, Julia had effectively imagined that she was everything to her mother, but she had then brutally discovered that this woman had no memory of it. Furthermore, she must have realized that her father occupied a bigger place in the grand scheme than she did because he was able to make the family bigger. It would not be at all strange if Julia, having been evicted from her position, suffered from a simple case of jealousy. But the dramatic annihilation of her identity necessitated that I consider other factors.

In order to survive the failings of her parents, Julia had become a big girl too quickly and must have prematurely acquired adult means of survival. Her walls of protection had thus gotten bigger in order for her to live while sheltering her mother in her little girl's bosom. If Julia envied something, it was not therefore my big office, but all these big things that she had equipped herself with to come to her mother's aid, and that had been swept aside by the latter's inability to recognize them.

Envy is triggered when an essential fantasy is annihilated. Such a fantasy is fundamental because, by placing itself between the child and her terrors, it permits an individual to acquire the tools to make up for the deficiencies of those surrounding her. Through this fantasy, where a child imagines the ways she fills a void in her parent's desire, life's experiences are organized and have meaning. This vital construction had been destroyed by her mother's infantile laughter. Deprived of this indispensable point of reference, Julia had lost all consistency, collapsing into a vacant space where she was no longer anything or anyone.

ENVY AND JEALOUSY

Envy stands in the way of fruitful exchanges with others. It prevents a person from reaching out. In Julia's case, my office stood for everything of which she felt deprived. No common space was henceforth possible. The envious character, thus deprived, contemplated the other shore with rage and bitterness. It became an Eden from which she was separated and where, in her eyes, all the goods were found. It was Julia's envy that established me as inhuman in my big office, and not some other desirable object in my possession. In doing this, she cut herself off from me, ousting me and my analytic compass. "Who do you think you are?" she had thrown at me, forgetting all my efforts to help her and thinking that I did not belong to the same world as she did.

Envy comes along in defense, as a response to the amputation of a part of one's self. We can thus understand why this means of defense is so alienating and regressive.

Different from the jealous individual who suffers a thousand ills, the envious person gags and smothers the pain caused by an insoluble identity conflict. Deprived of the sense of her existence,

Julia wanted to put another under the same spell; her covetousness had no other goal than to lower me to the status of a vulgar thing. Hence the choice of my big office, the coveted object, cropped up again and again to obliterate the quality of our work together.

Envy is considered the passion behind hatred. It is catastrophic and, to a certain extent, comparable to autism. Julia placed us in two different and impermeable worlds. Her hatred constituted an autistic shell, and because of it she became inaccessible, cold, and inhuman. Reality was from this point onward frozen in a sort of timelessness. Thus she willingly affirmed that her envy was born from indisputable facts existing from time immemorial. She didn't want to know anything about the common space that linked her to other people. She couldn't face the fact that she wanted something from me. I had become confused with my office that was too big.

In a person's development, envy emerges later than jealousy. The envious person does not regress to an infantile stage. Rather she denies the tools she had at her disposal growing up, frozen in a place where she can't see that what she yearns for is something she once had. Yet having been cut off from landmarks that once gave her the experience of being wanted and loved, she is left with an envy for things, in place of actual relationships and human contact.

Locked up in her envious hatred, Julia could have continued to be indefinitely divided, condemning our relationship as she had all others. Her amorous and friendly ties, damaged by the past, would have continued to fuel her bitterness all the more if she had kept denying that which made her furious.

ACCEPTING THE ANALYST'S GIFT

In tears Julia began to recount the incessant changes that had occurred in her family. Julia had to endure her father's fits of anger because it was her job to shield the others from them. Rather than protecting Julia, her mother assumed that as the eldest she was in charge. Such a position caused her to be mocked and ridiculed by the entire family. Julia had to live in a landscape of perpetual betrayals. As a child, she could not understand that her mother was immature and irresponsible. She saw her as ungrateful and endowed with unlimited and arbitrary power. Her tears bore witness to the fact that she no longer had to deny all that she had endured.

In the past, in order to survive, Julia had taken on a role in which she was bigger than her mother; at least her mother needed her and this alone gave her a reason to live and feel strong. Her envious fits of rage were directly linked to the fact that she had sacrificed the image of herself as the big one for her mother. She had renounced this position without receiving any compensation.

The fact that my office was suddenly too big became clear through Julia's evocation of the changing dynamics of her family. The warping perimeters of my office walls became the metaphor of the nonsense into which she had been thrown. "If nothing is ever stable and all bearings permanently tumble down, there is nothing I can lean on!" Lost in her destructive rage, Julia could not hear the cries of her own confusion.

Julia was finally able to make use of our relationship when she consented to look beyond her rage and retrieve the big girl who had been so helpful to her growing up. With me, she could start healing the wound that had damaged her vision of herself before the birth of her sister. "Never again can anyone take away from me what is mine, or what is *in* me, or what *is* me," she then cried out. No one could deprive her of the means she had forged, received, and made her own.

From then on, because I was no longer the only one to hold the symbolic tools of a big person and we were able to share a common space, my presence was no longer so threatening and Julia became willing to reflect on her real expectations. Together we battled against the "horrible things in her head," those eruptions of chaos and pleasure through which her identity was lost. She modified her work life from top to bottom and took into account her own capacities that, until now, had similarly been denied and envied in others. With me at her side, Julia finally accepted the turmoil that had inhabited her until then. She could finally share with me a common symbolic space without the fear of having made it all up. Moreover she could even feel grateful, a sign that her previous split had been healed.

It is very disconcerting for an analyst to have her urge to give be fought with such determination while the person in her presence is there precisely to receive that gift. But giving alone does not suffice as long as the *space of giving* does not exist. It is this symbolic space that the analysis restores, distinguishing it from other forms of behavioral or empathic therapy. Envy is witness to the fact that the space of giving has been wounded, meaning it is not so much a destructive tendency as an alienating and regressive defense.

Contrary to jealousy, which is a pain that surges again and again, envy tends to eradicate pain that cannot be contained or tolerated. Thus the envious person is spared of suffering. Having stripped herself of the means with which to face her distress, the envious person is relieved in the immediate present. But being violently cut off from herself, Julia's relief became laced with bitterness upon seeing others who delight in less rigid ties than her own. She was bad tempered without knowing why. She was unaware that she had to resort to such a defense mechanism in order to act and be an actor in her life.

Working with the envious patient puts a special demand on the analyst. She must be able to enter into the terrain of the envious person's ruined world, meet her, and hear her from that place. This requires staying power, for sure, but also the understanding that the analyst must inhabit this destroyed world with the patient at least for a moment. There the analyst will find the traces of a lost individual. Being given permission to love herself again through the eyes of another, Julia found that her envied objects started losing their appeal.

CHAPTER 10

GEORGE: THE MAN WHO WAS JEALOUS OF FLOWERS

George always seemed oblivious. No matter what subject was broached, his tone of voice displayed a marked indifference. Paid to listen to him, I felt reduced to a function, a bureaucrat of sorts; he was the 6:30 PM patient, nothing more. George decided to seek help because he had started to drink alone recently and didn't want to get trapped in an alcoholism that reminded him of his sad and solitary existence. A man in his late forties, George had very little in his life except his work as a financial analyst in a bank. When he complained during his sessions, he did so mainly about his boss, an irritable man like his own father, similarly "hard and cold" and with whom he had had a relationship based on submission and silent revolt. When I suggested that he take note of the curious anonymity that he condemned me to when I tried to engage him, he burst out laughing. "Why should I bother questioning myself about that?" he retorted, incapable of noticing the mute violence to which he submitted me.

One day, however, he noticed the vase of flowers that stood as usual on the table in my office. Why did he notice them on this day? Were there more flowers this time, were they more colorful, more fragrant? I don't know. George marveled on seeing them, asked me about them, and flared up with anger on learning that these flowers had always been there, under his nose, and that he probably had never noticed them before. He seemed offended. Scandalously indifferent to him, the flowers had taken the liberty of existing without his authorization. What's more, they allowed themselves to be looked at by me, by others, strangers, independent of his presence and even without him. He was shocked by the invasion of a world that he no longer mastered. "You're crazy about these flowers!" he exclaimed, looking alarmed.

Soon, however, he was quick to ridicule my bouquets and to imagine that some grateful patient offered me flowers by way of payment. I pointed out that he, at least, didn't bring me flowers! In his choked little laugh, I saw that I had hit home. He began to direct his anger at me, his father, his superior, all those who, he asserted, conned him.

Beyond George's feelings of persecution, I sensed a serious anger raging against any infraction to his well-organized world. Had the invasion of a few flowers endangered his life? What was the meaning, I wondered, of this sudden outburst of jealousy toward a simple bouquet? This man's obsessive tendencies revealed an incredible fragility. His difficulties with his superiors were a cover for a void.

George didn't compliment anyone, with bunches of flowers or otherwise. He didn't like many people, lived quite a solitary life, and asserted loudly and strongly that he didn't suffer because of it. As no one found favor in his eyes, he felt justified in not trying to seduce anyone. For him, women were an unpredictable source of disagreements; he had renounced pleasing them. On the subject of his relationships, he didn't "play into overtime," he said, and he left his women without any apparent regret once the relationship had been hastily consummated.

From what I could make out, he seemed to get real satisfaction in making them jealous once he left them.

Abandoned by his mother when he was five years old (she had chosen her career over him, he had been told), he justified his indifference and his desire to get revenge on women. "You women, you hide your game well" he liked to say to me. The flowers, too, hid their game, I thought. My bouquets had invaded his space and thrown off his equilibrium. A few flowers were enough to force George to withdraw. They no doubt evoked for him my sexual otherness. Women were inscrutable for George.

JEALOUSY OF THE FEMININE

The feminine world associated with these flowers became, henceforth, the object of intense interrogations. Who was sending me these flowers, George wondered. A lover, a husband? From one week to the next he couldn't stop himself from comparing the bouquets. He laughed when they weren't particularly luxurious, scoffed with a certain virulence when they were abundant. He rid me of all doubt as to his jealousy of a rival the day when, convinced that no lover would have sent me flowers so assiduously, he spoke of his satisfaction that I alone provided myself with flowers. His relief was of short duration.

"Where did I find such strange flowers?" he asked. "How did I manage to think of them every week?" He would have liked, he said to me one day, to put some flowers in his own office, "but it would look a bit strange for a man, wouldn't it?" he thought. "Would [he] not be taken for a homosexual?" he added. The analysis had certainly gotten some color back into it, but I began to dread the moment that I put out a new bouquet, feeling constantly surveyed, stripped bare. I had wanted to stop being just a part of the décor. And I'd succeeded: he never took his eyes off me! I thought I was invisible for him, both as his analyst and as a woman, but now he tracked my every move. George couldn't bear the thought that I delighted in picking my flowers every week, a pleasure he clearly couldn't control, but one he envied and therefore needed to thwart.

He was eager to control my frivolity, my madness, my desire, which were all three identical in his eyes. An unvoiced violence agitated our session on one occasion. Scared but attracted by all aspects of my femininity, he was both thirsty for my attention and resentful for wanting to seek it. He could only reject what he craved to approach.

My bouquets also evoked the changing moods that he attributed to every woman, and particularly to his mother. He had been kept at a distance from her "for his own good," he was told by his father's side of the family. Up to that point we spoke only of the heroism of this father who brought him up alone "the hard way," with the help of his grandmother, and far away from a woman who was exclusively worried about her career. The family fairy tale that George portrayed was about to collapse.

REDISCOVERING THE COLORS OF A MOTHER'S LOVE

Having recently started working in the art world, George often described certain paintings that he liked. He was particularly keen on paintings with flowers. Was George expressing a need to appeal to my tastes in order to please me or was this a demonstration of his anguish over the idea of separating from me? He offered eulogies when the time neared to change my flowers, and this evoked for me the image of an anxious child who runs under his mother's skirt to keep her for one moment longer.

Seeing how meticulously he described my flowers gave me the impression, I told him, of a painter who wanted to fix the image for eternity on a more solid and less transient easel than the ephemeral artworks of our sessions. "I cannot hear your words," he shouted, "they are just noise in my head." Then he added, seized with panic, "It's like the air is cut in two when you speak."

On hearing him talk about "noise," I calculated just how intense his terror must have been when he separated from his mother. Perhaps I hadn't been attentive enough to a slight, somewhat defensive movement of mine when faced with his burning desire to inhale my femininity up close. He showed me how sensitive he was to the slightest of my retreats. His anguish meant that language lost all meaning when she disappeared. He was prey to a great fear that his bond with me and with words would be destroyed, "cut in two."

Behind the adult who scrutinized my bouquets, there was the scared child who didn't know if, like my flowers, I would remain the same at each of our meetings or if I would appear changed, different and unpredictable like the bouquets. "That child in you, forgotten by everyone, speaks out today to say that he doesn't know where he is any longer when he's alone or when he sees his mother again after her absences," I said to him one day.

The expression "the air is cut in two" signified for him that a gulf lay between us. My words, however, managed to throw a bridge between the two edges of the precipice. I noted also that the words had a calming effect on him. "I was told that my mother had left because she wanted to be a star at the opera. I didn't know what that meant. I used to gaze into the evening sky for a long time to try and find her. She was a shooting star, yes! She came to see me and then disappeared very quickly, dressed in beautiful robes of all colors." I didn't realize that by proposing the image of our sessions as changing artworks I would cause him to tumble yet again into a place where the meaning of words and of life was already damaged.

Obliged to sever himself from his desire to see his mother in order to conform to his father's dictates, he was cured of the desire, but only at the price of a terrible mutilation of his existence. His jealousy of my femininity was in proportion to how he had been deprived of it. My flowers, symbolic of the maternal colors, had been reduced in his life to nothing for a long time. He had been forbidden to think about them. Perhaps his mother's colored robes were rediscovered in the varied corollas of my flowers.

"When I was a child, gazing at the stars, I had imagined that the moon was a medallion in the sky, that showed me alone, the photo of my mother. On the hidden face of the moon, there must have been the face of a dead person, I thought. Once, when I saw my mother again, her face had changed, it was puffy, bizarre, a moon, yes . . . a moon face," he said to me later on. We could thus begin to trace the constellation of his mother's reality. Gravely depressed (her depression and the antidepressants had given her this moon face), she had fought to keep her son, but had been pushed aside by the father's family who were delighted to have an heir. His mother's German origins were an insult and embarrassment to this French family. George had literally been abducted by his father and his grandmother under the pretext of this woman's fragility. She was described to the child as inconstant, fickle, and unbalanced. In fact, they had carried out, after the war, a sort of ethnic cleansing. She had since returned to her country of origin, and they hadn't heard from her since. By rediscovering traces of her, George could confirm our hypothesis that his mother had not willingly abandoned him. And the hidden face of the moon stopped being the face of someone whose traces he had wiped out.

His father's behavior had prevented George from keeping alive in his memories the image of his mother and his tie to her.

Deprived of the hope of reestablishing a bridge between his mother's and father's worlds, he had taken it upon himself to be strong. He had tried to construct a semblance of masculinity, imitating his father's heroism and building upon the devaluation and eradication of the maternal feminine. Confronted by distressing enigmas, a child doesn't know if his terror is justified or not. When he feels an incomprehensible hatred toward a loved one, he loses his own identity. George felt himself become a shooting star when he thought about his family's hatred of his mother, because he felt "cut in two." Because his family had rejected her so completely, this was his attempt to keep his mother alive in his memories. George was not given permission to be schooled in feminine delights, through his mother's beauty and talent. He too became a shooting star every time he attempted to rescue his connection to the maternal and its nourishment for his starved self.

My playing with the different meanings of the word "shot" had roused a violent rupture in him, insurmountable and painful. The cry with which he enunciated this intimate catastrophe allowed him to clamber out of a subjective experience that had been lived until then in abysmal solitude. Through a legitimate jealousy animated in him by my bunches of flowers, he contemplated the unfathomable enigma that I had ended up embodying. His jealousy of my flowers had been a benefit: a self stripped of flowers had thus been able to remind us of his mother's presence. He was able to retrieve both his memories of his mother—who was deprived of her maternal rights and femininity—and of himself, who was deprived of maternal love and attention.

Reassured and more collected because he no longer had any grounds to deny his terror about the feminine, George set out to construct a more lasting attachment with a woman whom he had recently met and liked. I listened to him, interested by his new emotions, evoke the inebriating perfume of his new companion, the trouble that grabbed hold of him when her body opened itself up to him like a blooming corolla, the anguish that gripped him at the thought of losing himself in a sexual pleasure that was too intense, too new, too different from what he had previously experienced.

BREAKING THE SHACKLES OF DESIRE

Suddenly, my flowers stopped pleasing him. For some time, he confessed, he was filled with a desire to throw the vase in my face, to smash it and above all to stamp on the flowers; I filled it too regularly for his liking. Was this a case of an upsurge of jealousy? Everything indicated as much, especially when I heard him conclude, "Even if the world collapsed, you'd still only be worried about your flowers!"

However this wasn't a fit of jealousy. He was no longer (as he had been) a shattered vase awaiting a bouquet, deprived of the flowers of attention of a mother indifferent to his collapsed world. He could not freely love the other sex as long as a flaw inside of him continued to thwart his impulses toward the world. The two elements, vase and flowers, in their multiple incarnations had served their purpose. They were now—thanks to the maternal and feminine support of his analyst—linked to a fantasy that made it possible for George to encounter a woman. His internal split stitched up, he was no longer obliged to put masculine and feminine masks onto his fellow creatures. As his outburst illustrated, he was animated by a healthy anger that did not crush him, that no longer shattered him. He no longer needed me to stick the pieces together like a too-good mother, so he tested me to see if I was jealous of his freedom.

To want to break a tie, even a benevolent one, is a way of pitting oneself against it, of recognizing it, of making it one's own. This appropriation is not done without violence, I told him. He wanted to be free to love or not, and to be alone to decide it. He wanted to confront the challenge of love on his own; for this reason, the purely benevolent presence of his analyst was pernicious. He needed, alone, to dispel the distressing nonsense that the other sex represented in order to decide to love it. We must all, at some time or another, confront our solitude before the strangeness of sexuality. George thus wanted a solitude no longer imposed, but assumed.

A few months after George expressed his wish to be free, he told me he had remained pensive for several hours after that session, had sat on a bench in a square, thinking of his lover, troubled as if submerged by a great emotion. He had rediscovered the unfathomable charm of feminine desire within the very same impulse where I had recognized his thirst for solitude and liberty. Authorized to smash the vase of domination and of hatred toward the maternal—as all boys growing up need to do— he had also broken this feminine emblem in order to symbolically seize hold of it. For this to come to pass, it was appropriate that I be neither broken by his desire for liberty, nor jealous of it.

Is George's profound bewilderment and jealousy toward femininity an accident linked to his own family history, or does it refer to a pervasive mentality in our culture? It is not uncommon, in the societies in which we live, to associate what pertains to the feminine with dismissive statements pointing to women's fickleness, unreliability, or inferior status. Although the women's movement has certainly abated overtly dismissive social attitudes toward women, it has been unable or maybe unwilling to address what is really at stake: the enigma of the feminine and the power that seems to be associated with it. If George's case is emblematic of such fear, it also points to a flaw that even our postmodern societies have not been able to mend: There is no legitimate slot, in our language or in our institutions, that allows for a boy or a girl to acknowledge and enjoy the feminine dimension of their mother's being.

THE FEAR OF DESIRE AS UNFATHOMABLE

A boy deprived of maternal identification as George was suffers as a result of the grave amputation of a part of himself. He endures this deprivation as if it is inflicted by his father's tyrannical cruelty; the violence is all the more terrifying when it seems to make no sense to the child. He does not understand that the adult—in this case his father—is subjected to his own fear of the maternal enigma, which he likewise developed toward his mother while growing up. As a result, the father too can behave like a cruel little king, playing a role very different than a son may expect from a father. George's father, for example, had rejected his wife and her cultural heritage with the support of his family—a clear indication that it was as a son, not as a man, that he had broken all ties with the feminine enigma his wife represented. George's condescending and dismissive attitude toward his analyst and women in general did not only stem from his identification with his father, but also appeared at first as a conventional masculine strategy to keep at bay the pernicious representation of maternal power pervasive in our society.

This all-powerfulness projected onto mothers is in turn envied, imitated, and perpetuated in a terrible vicious circle. In other words, the dangerous power attributed to mothers needs to be fenced off by the ideal of male domination. In this scenario, a son's relationship to his mother's femininity can only be vilified and denigrated. When society does not acknowledge the benefits of a son's identification with his mother's feminine qualities, and the father perpetuates such interdiction, the child cannot hold on to a maternal image to sustain his capacity to love as an autonomous being. The child, like George growing up, lives in fear of being accused of being weak. If the bouquet of flowers had not revealed the drama lurking underneath George's conventional vision of women's unpredictable desire, he would have remained a man unable to reach out to the other sex.

It is therefore crucial that society acknowledge that women's sexual desire is as varied and complex as that of men. The more the feminine Eros is negated, the more it is identified with figures of castrating mothers or something equally pernicious.

When a woman cannot celebrate her own sex's eroticism before her children (either because she feels excluded and held in contempt, or because she experiences her own sexuality with profound anxiety), this dimension seems all the more terrifying or wild for her son or her daughter. It becomes impossible for the child to integrate this feminine dimension. George, deprived of the joys of his mother's femininity, became obsessed with the only sign that reminded him of her. He lacked not only the loving presence of his mother but also the possibility of identifying with some of her qualities. Before his analysis recovered them as stable representations, fine art, stars, and colorful flowers had been sad or threatening symbols circling meaninglessly around him.

Therefore it is the feminine Eros that alone can humanize the maternal, providing a barrier between mothers and sons, more effective and appealing than the so-called prohibition of incest imposed by a father on his son. In other words, it is as much the mother's place as the father's to transmit to their sons what is a woman, therefore allowing the boy to accommodate in his fantasy not only that which is forbidden but also that which he may be able to internalize as his own. Not all that is feminine should be excluded from the boy's elaboration of his masculine identity.

Due to his lack of identification with the symbolic values of his mother, George imitated the traits of virility rather than enjoying them. Incapable of truly loving, such men are envious and jealous of the feminine, which represents, through what is projected on it, a liberty of desire that they do not have. This is how jealousy toward women is transmitted in an infernal vicious circle.

SOLITUDE, LOVE, DEATH

Isn't it a paradox that our human sexuality still eludes us? Not exclusively determined by our hormones, it escapes language's attempts to circumscribe it. However much it uses the tools of fantasy to transform the effects of archaic joys or terrors into pleasure, it never manages to do so perfectly. Thus, a part of sexuality escapes all mechanical control and leaves each person alone before it. Paradoxically however, it can also become the place for transforming one's fear, through the anxiety of desire, into pleasure.

It is clearly a misconception to assume that mothers resist severing ties with their children. Every time a woman brings a child into the world, her love implies the urge to separate from him as well as to connect. A mother is also a woman with other interests than her children. She discovers that to separate from her children is part and parcel of her love and sense of responsibility toward her offspring.

THE LIBERTY OF EROS

Society organizes for us "roles" that we must occupy as woman or man. These roles are useful insofar as they allow us to lean on them when we attempt to make sense of sexual urges that often take us by surprise. But the way society seems to set in stone the differences between the sexes can also have traumatic effects, as George's plight illustrates. George had been cut off not only from maternal love but also from the pleasures of basking in his mother's femininity. He needed to recapture a taste of this lost paradise to feel free to love and desire, no longer constrained by the arbitrary edicts that a man must be strong and that a woman is either a whore or a good mother. Femininity as elusive and unforeseen should not be the exclusive property of women. Men too should be allowed, even encouraged, to explore the limits of their masculine self and venture into feminine territory. There are no fixed recipes to love as a man or as a woman. Neither the masculine nor the feminine possesses in itself the impossible liberty to control desire, but both embody it in their own way. When men and women yield to the fleetingness of desire, only then can they have the delicious illusion of reinventing themselves and each other.

BEYOND JEALOUSY

"How to live?" remained, for a long time, the question patients most frequently asked psychoanalysts. Are we conflicted, they asked, because we can't figure out what we want or because we feel constrained by obstacles that we can't overcome? Behind this question, though, lurks another: It is no longer "how to live" that is the object of patients' questioning, but rather "where to live." Jealous individuals are paradigmatic of this type of contemporary distress. They are homeless beings, cut off from themselves. It is not only mentally ill people who live painfully exiled elsewhere. Jealous people are also driven outside themselves by their passion, desperately seeming to ask, "Where can I live without shelter and without the home base that gives me a stable identity?"

Lacking landmarks that would provide a mental place to live, the jealous individual teeters at the edge of failure and breakdown. "Am I myself or am I this other who goes off with a part of me? Am I loved or am I repelled?" he relentlessly asks himself. Jealousy places the individual in an impossible place, a nonspace in which he tries to constitute himself as an individual, while at the same time finding himself excluded from the outside world. Jealousy at once conceals and exposes the terror and the suffering of abandonment; it is linked to a flaw at the heart of a person's identity.

The most common form of jealousy has the jealous person believing he is surrounded by men and women who are other to him, who live in a different world and have nothing in common with him. He often envisions them with powers he believes he doesn't possess. Searching for rivals whom he can't find, he wavers, incapable of confronting the uncertainties of desire. Believing that the cause and thus the illusory solution of his suffering lies in his rival, he is not aware that this very image that he creates to give shape to his worry serves to alienate him all the more.

It is only when he relinquishes his jealousy that the jealous individual, recognizing in his rival a fellow creature like himself, can demystify those powers that he has attributed to him. At last accepting the human condition, made up of fragile identities, trembling emotions, and unwarranted uncertainties, he is able to understand that his suffering was not in fact governed by some villainous plot. Taking into account his own fragility, as well as the fragility of those around him, makes it possible for him to acquit those he loves of his endless charges of infidelity.

All of this shows us how male and female rivals and lovers, by providing the jealous man or woman with the opportunity to assume the posture of victim, likewise permit them to divide the world into martyrs of betrayal (themselves) and torturers of hearts. Such a vision of the world is very alienating and rigid. The jealous person seems unable to identify with anyone. With an implacable constancy, his rivals or lovers sooner or later seem strange, inaccessible, and ultimately pernicious to him.

This has ethical and political implications. Through the flaw in his own identity, the jealous person displays how much every other person who is in his field of vision is placed far away from him, offstage, beyond ties. The ethical question—the status of the other—finds its political consequence in working out how to diminish the distance that jealousy puts between oneself and the other.

Here is where the art of the psychoanalyst comes into play. Depending on a loved one whom he no longer trusts, jealous individuals invite their psychoanalyst to imagine the unliveable position in which they stay despite themselves. For jealous men and women, the analyst does not only stand as a character in their story. Analysis also locates the patient and the analyst amid all the words and images of a childhood language that the patient has been stripped of or that he lacks. The analyst inhabits this wounded space, lending the person images, limits, and faults, so that he may loosen the muzzles of his childhood language and be allowed to express his craving for love and his need to have his vulnerability acknowledged.

If psychoanalysts and patients are similarly subject to the vagaries of the heart, their respective positions are not the same. This fact, however, does not deny the difficult path of reciprocity that is indispensable in psychoanalysis, especially for those who live outside themselves. In order to find a solution to the painful oscillation that plagues jealous men and women, the person listening to them has to be willing to voyage with them in a jealous boat, rocky and unpredictable. It is uniquely under this condition that the jealous person can risk letting go of the mirages of his imaginary rivals, who condemn him to hunting for signs of infidelity in those he loves.

The jealous person is not up to separating himself from the objects of his quest. Unable to truly love or hate, he can't detach himself from the objects of his love or of his jealousy. When there is a fixation, an impossibility of loving or separating, it is the whole force of the childhood language that is paralyzed. The goal then is to restore the feelings and words associated with these childhood experiences that had been gagged by anxiety. Brought back to life, childhood can then express itself in the adult, to his great profit. When, thanks to his analysis, the jealous person rediscovers his impulses, without a sense of guilt, he has discovered that his destructivity wasn't as lethal as he dreaded, that his loves survive it—and his analyst as well.

The question "where to live?" presupposes the existence of uninhabitable places that the psychoanalyst has learned to explore. Jealousy is a case in point. The question of the unliveable obliges the practitioner to imagine and to put herself into these places that she does not know. It is up to the psychoanalyst to construct with her patient a space where the possibility of an encounter with a fellow creature develops. In other words, this comes down to building with him the empty, undetermined space of his predisposition to love, and to avoid saturating it with declarations of good intentions. The consequences of psychoanalysis go far beyond its practice. As analysts, we think and search to construct a space where two fellow creatures can be together. What more burning ethical and political issue could there be?